Reminisce

CHRISTMAS

table of contents

REMINISCE CHRISTMAS
Julie Kastello Editor
Angela Packer Art Director
Ken Wysocky, John Rech, Ann Wilson, Shannon Somers-Mueller Contributors
Deb Warlaumont Mulvey Copy Chief
Trudi Bellin Photo Coordinator
Joanne Weintraub, Dulcie Shoener, Marybeth Jacobson Copy Editors
Dena Ahlers Layout Designer
Mary Ann Koebernik Assistant Photo Coordinator

Bettina Miller Editor, *Reminisce*
Cheryl A. Michalek Art Director, *Reminisce*
John Burlingham Associate Editor, *Reminisce*
Blanche Comiskey, Melody Trick Editorial Assistants, *Reminisce*

Catherine Cassidy VP/Editor-in-Chief
Heather Lamb Executive Editor
Sharon K. Nelson Creative Director
Rachael Liska Product Development Editor

Lisa Karpinski North American Chief Marketing Officer

THE READER'S DIGEST ASSOCIATION, INC.
Mary G. Berner President and Chief Executive Officer
Suzanne M. Grimes President, North American Affinities

The Most Wonderful Time...

Every year when the calendar flips to December, I find myself feeling lighthearted. Excitement builds each day as I hear holiday tunes on the radio and watch TV favorites like *How the Grinch Stole Christmas!* and *Rudolph, the Red-Nosed Reindeer.*

Once again, boxes of familiar ornaments and a cherished Nativity set are brought up from the basement, and evenings at home seem more special in the warm glow of Christmas tree lights. At this point, I'm even likely to burst into song: *It's the most—wonderful—time—of the year!*

Over the decades, Christmas changes for each of us. As children, we feel the magic. Santa is real, cookies and candy are everywhere, and the anticipation of opening gifts on Christmas morning is nearly impossible to bear. It just doesn't get much better.

As we grow up, holidays come with more responsibility. Young parents are now the ones making magical memories for their children. Days grow hectic with shopping, parties and travel plans to be with family or friends.

One thing that never changes, though, is the pure joy of remembering Christmas past: family traditions, letters to Santa, singing with the church choir, organizing special meals and gifts for neighbors in need. Thoughts of long-ago feasting at Grandma and Grandpa's house become precious as generations change and so many are no longer with us.

Many people now have gone back to simpler celebrations that focus more on the true meaning of Christmas and less on expensive presents. Sharing fond memories of seasons past with family and friends is a priceless gift, whether it's over coffee at the kitchen table or via card, phone or e-mail.

The stories and photos in this book were shared by *Reminisce* readers and are sure to touch the heart. We've also included space to write down your own Christmas memories, creating a personal keepsake of lasting value.

NOW CAN I OPEN IT?
I was about 6 when Dad took this photo on Christmas Eve in the late '60s.

Merry Christmas to you all,

Bettina Miller

Bettina Miller
Editor, *Reminisce* magazine

5

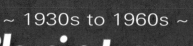

Christmas
through the years

The Christmases that live in our memories center on family and faith. But how we choose to celebrate the season has been shaped by the world events that have happened around us. Economic times affected the gifts we found under our trees, for example, while pop culture determined if we sang along with Bing or mimicked the falsetto of Alvin and the Chipmunks. Here's a look at the special events, sights and sounds that have shaped the season as we each know, and remember, it.

1930s

1931 The Coca-Cola Santa, depicted by artist Haddon Sundblom as a jolly man in a red suit, debuts in advertising in the *Saturday Evening Post*. The ensuing ads shape the way we see Santa today.

1933 The Radio City Christmas Spectacular, featuring the Rockettes, "The Parade of the Wooden Soldiers" and "The Living Nativity," makes its debut in New York. The eight-week run of shows has been sold out every year since.

▶ **1934** The Ideal Novelty Toy Corp. introduces the Shirley Temple doll, dressed to match costumes the young actress wore in her movies. Mint-condition dolls in the original box have sold for more than $1,000.

The first Mickey Mouse balloon appears in the Macy's Thanksgiving Day Parade. It remains a parade favorite.

1935 Monopoly, a board game invented by Charles B. Darrow of Germantown, Pennsylvania, is the best-selling game in America its first year on the market.

▶ **1937** Max Eckhardt, an importer of hand-blown glass Christmas ornaments from Germany, founds the Shiny Brite company, which mass-produces glass ornaments by adapting the manufacturing process used for lightbulbs. The ornaments are decorated by hand.

▶ **1938** A film version of Charles Dickens' *A Christmas Carol* starring Reginald Owen as Ebenezer Scrooge is released.

1939 Robert L. May, a copywriter for Chicago-based Montgomery Ward & Co., originates the character Rudolph the Red-Nosed Reindeer in a story written for a promotional giveaway.

The Daisy Red Ryder BB gun—which will forever be linked with Christmas through the writings of Jean Shepherd and the 1983 movie *A Christmas Story*—is introduced.

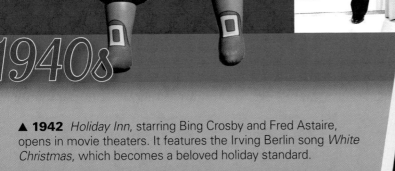

1940s

▲ **1942** *Holiday Inn*, starring Bing Crosby and Fred Astaire, opens in movie theaters. It features the Irving Berlin song *White Christmas*, which becomes a beloved holiday standard.

1942-'44 Macy's suspends its Thanksgiving Day Parade and deflates its balloons, donating 650 pounds of scrap rubber to the war effort.

1944 Inspired by second-graders in Smithtown, New York, Donald Yetter Gardner writes the novelty song *All I Want for Christmas Is My Two Front Teeth*.

▶ **1945** Inventor Richard James and his wife, Betty, sell out of their first 400 Slinkys in 90 minutes at Gimbels Department Store in Philadelphia. Since then, more than 300 million have been sold.

1946 Singer Nat King Cole records *The Christmas Song*, by Mel Torme and Bob Wells. Most people recognize it by its opening line: "Chestnuts roasting on an open fire …"

▲ **1947** The Macy's Thanksgiving Day Parade is broadcast on national television for the first time. Now more than 50 million viewers tune in to watch this kickoff to the holiday season.

▶ The movie *Miracle on 34th Street*, starring Maureen O'Hara, Natalie Wood and Edmund Gwenn, is released.

The first Tonka brand metal toy trucks—a steam shovel and a crane—roll off the assembly line in Mound, Minnesota. Today, the distinctive yellow trucks remain a sandbox standard.

1949 Gene Autry releases his recording of *Rudolph the Red-Nosed Reindeer*, written by Johnny Marks. It sells 2.5 million copies its first year.

▶ Milton Bradley begins producing Candy Land, a game invented by Eleanor Abbot of San Diego to entertain children affected by polio. The "sweet little game … for sweet little folks" has been a part of childhood ever since.

Christmas Through the Years

1950s

▲ **1952** Hasbro starts selling Mr. Potato Head, a toy that includes the parts for fashioning a face but requires children to supply their own potatoes. A plastic potato was added to the kit in 1964. In 2000, Mr. P.H. was inducted into the Toy Hall of Fame.

1953 President Dwight D. Eisenhower and his wife, Mamie, send the first U.S. presidential Christmas cards. At the time, a stamp cost 3 cents.

▶ **1954** Capitalizing on the popularity of the song *White Christmas*, Paramount Pictures releases a movie of the same name starring Bing Crosby and Danny Kaye. It is the highest-grossing film that year and remains a seasonal favorite.

1957 Random House publishes *How the Grinch Stole Christmas!* by Dr. Seuss. Reading the classic children's book continues to be a holiday tradition generation after generation.

▶ Elvis Presley launches a rock 'n' roll holiday classic when he records *Blue Christmas* by Bill Hayes and Jay Johnson for *Elvis' Christmas Album*.

1958 The aluminum Christmas tree is introduced. More than a million trees are welcomed into American homes until they fall out of favor in the mid-1960s.

The Chipmunk Song (Christmas Don't Be Late), a novelty number by Ross Bagdasarian (aka David Seville) that pays tribute to a popular toy that year, the hula hoop, becomes a hit for Alvin and the Chipmunks.

Brenda Lee records *Rockin' Around the Christmas Tree*, composed by Johnny Marks.

▶ **1959** Mattel introduces the Barbie doll. Today, thousands of girls a year will find her under the tree.

1960 Ohio Art Co. begins producing the Etch A Sketch. The red-framed gray screen remains a cornerstone of the activity aisle at toy stores.

▲ **1962** The animated TV special *Mr. Magoo's Christmas Carol*, a musical adaptation of the Dickens story with the title character voiced by Jim Backus, airs for the first time.

1963 Kenner Products' Easy-Bake Oven, America's first working toy oven, begins selling at $15.95. After many revisions, the classic is brought back in 2007 and today retails at $25.99.

▲ **1964** Bob Hope takes his USO Christmas show to Vietnam for the first time.

▶ The animated TV special *Rudolph the Red-Nosed Reindeer*, featuring the singing of Burl Ives, premieres. It has been telecast every year since, introducing new generations to the reindeer with the glowing nose and an elf named Hermey who wants to be a dentist.

Hasbro's G.I. Joe arrives in stores. With its moving parts, the action figure continues to offer boys opportunities for interactive play and make-believe mayhem.

▶ **1965** The animated TV special *A Charlie Brown Christmas*, based on the *Peanuts* strip by Charles M. Schulz and featuring the music of the Vince Guaraldi Trio, is broadcast for the very first time.

▶ **1966** *How the Grinch Stole Christmas!* becomes an animated special narrated by Boris Karloff. Initially receiving mixed reviews, it's now generally considered a holiday classic.

1967 *Christmas With the King Family* features a surprise reunion between singer Alyce King and her son Ric, who'd been serving in the military.

1969 The Macy's Thanksgiving Day Parade includes floats for the first time.

CHAPTER ONE

Family Traditions

Few holidays resonate with more traditions than Christmas. Whether it's baking and decorating cookies, singing joyous carols, driving around town to see who outdid themselves with outdoor decorations, or trying to take that perfect annual Christmas card family photo, customs and rituals abound.

Joanne Weber of Irvine, California (shown at top in 1957 with her late husband, Wayne Pevehouse, and children Tom and Debbie), says she always looked forward to decorating a tree, which fairly dripped with glittering tinsel.

For other families, the holiday wouldn't be the same without a special story. After hanging stockings and putting out Santa's snack, the Robinsons (center, from left, Jennifer, Heather and Angela) loved to hear father Evan read Clement C. Moore's classic "The Night Before Christmas," writes their mother, Lorraine, of Regina, Saskatchewan.

The same held true for the Beltz children, who would listen as their mother, Rosemary, read them the story of "Rudolph the Red-Nosed Reindeer," says daughter Deanna Harmon of Goodyear, Arizona. She snapped this photo (bottom) of her mom and younger siblings, Stephen and Trudy, in 1951 in Dennison, Illinois.

Turn the page for more heartwarming traditions.

a season to savor

By Barbara Strampe Gjertson
Janesville, Wisconsin

Some of my most cherished memories are of Christmas with my parents, Victor and Ruth Strampe, and my three sisters when I was growing up in the 1950s. As soon as the Thanksgiving turkey and trimmings were cleared from the table, we focused on Christmas.

Out came Mom's cookbook with all of our treasured family recipes. The next few weeks would find Mom and her helpers baking cookies and making candies. Among our favorites were frosted cutouts that we decorated with colored sugar and silver and multicolored nonpareils. Then there were almond-flavored spritz, rosettes, krumkakes, fudge, divinity and Knox dainties.

Often Mom would make something new. One year it was big red cinnamon lollipops; another year it was old-fashioned taffy. Oh, the fun times we had in that kitchen!

After much pestering by us girls, Mom and Dad would decide it was time to pick out our Christmas tree at one of the local tree lots. Dad would start the tree-trimming by stringing the multicolored lights and placing our angel tree topper in its place of honor. Next Mom would add the multicolored glass bead garland, and finally it was time for us to help. We would hang all the ornaments and always finish our beautiful tree off with a brand-new box or two of tinsel. According to Dad, the only right way to hang tinsel was one strand at a time. Do you know many strands are in one box of tinsel? We didn't think we'd ever get done.

For the next few weeks, my sisters and I would spend our spare time playing a Christmas tree game. One of us would name the colors of an ornament while the others tried to guess which one it was.

After the tree was decorated and the storage boxes put away, we would head for Dad's dresser to select stockings for Santa to fill. We always used Dad's gray-and-red hunting socks because they were the biggest socks in the house. We each tried to choose the longest stocking with the idea it would hold more. It didn't occur to us that Santa was fair—and even the sort of guy who

GREAT GIFTS Christmas 1952 was special for Vicki, Barbara and Jacqueline Strampe, who received walking dolls from Santa Claus (top center) and a playhouse (left and far left) made by their mother. Youngest sister Marlene (with Mom, top right, in 1960) got a doll for her first Christmas in 1957 (top left), and a play kitchen set a few years later (above).

wouldn't give us more just because we had a longer stocking.

On Christmas morning, the rule was no one could get up before the streetlights went out. We girls would sit on our beds watching out the window, and as soon as those lights went off, we flew into our parents' room. Then we ran to the living room, where we found the tree surrounded with gifts and all of our stockings overflowing.

We could always count on a few things in our stockings each year: a huge apple, a fragrant orange, a skinny box of thin mints, a package of bubble-bath beads and a small mesh bag of chocolate coins wrapped in gold foil. The rest of the stocking was filled with surprises.

Mom had a way of making Christmas big. Items we needed, such as winter coats, boots and pajamas, were saved to put under the tree.

Every Christmas was special when my sisters and I were growing up. Our parents taught us why we celebrated Christmas while letting us enjoy the Santa part, too.

Santa also would bring each of us two or three smaller toys and one large gift to share. One year we received a pingpong table, another year a toboggan. But the year that stands out is 1952, when Mom gave Santa a big helping hand.

With assistance from men in the shop at work, she constructed a playhouse out of wooden slats used for making porches and window shades. It was light green, with a door, windows and a red roof. It was collapsible, could be set up in minutes and was large enough for us all to fit inside.

Santa did his part by sneaking into our room and getting our table and chairs. He placed them inside the house and put our brand-new walking dolls at the table. He also set the table with a new set of dishes. That Christmas, we were so excited we barely knew what to do first!

Years later, when our youngest sister was 3, Santa brought her a kitchen set to go with the playhouse. Dad was Santa's big helper that year, with a few hours of assembly to his credit.

Every Christmas was special when my sisters and I were growing up. Our parents taught us why we celebrated Christmas while letting us enjoy the Santa part, too. We had Christmas programs at church and school, and we made our annual drive to downtown Janesville to see all the holiday lights and decorations.

The years have passed and the playhouse, walking dolls and even the Christmas ornaments are gone. But my sisters—Jacqueline Strampe, Vicki Strampe Neumueller and Marlene Strampe Cornwell—and I have passed on these special family traditions.

Our children and grandchildren always hang their stockings and come over to bake and decorate cookies with us each year. We all get together to make Mom's Christmas dinner. And each family has started its own special traditions. This is what I believe holds us all together.

waiting for St. Nicholas

When you grow up in a big family, you learn to take turns, even when it's time to hang up your Christmas stocking. The children of William and Florence Eardly, wearing matching pajamas, did just that in a photo that appeared on page 1 of the *Dayton* (Ohio) *Herald* on Dec. 24, 1945. Mike, who now lives in Beaverton, Michigan, says the family eventually grew to 12 children, who are now scattered throughout the country. In 1945, the family included (from left) Mike, Tom, Patty Lou, Don, Mary Theresa, Florence and Gerry.

season's greetings

Sending warm holiday wishes to friends and family remains a time-honored tradition in which even the youngest in the family can participate. These cards sent in the 1940s show a skiing Santa, colorful bells, cute animals and a sweet little girl. The lovely lady with the packages sports the fashions of the decade, while the airliner flying over a snowy village heralds the future of travel.

the
SEASON'S
GREETINGS

Merry Christmas

Season's Greetings

Christmas Wishes

Happy Holidays

HAPPY CHRISTMAS GREETINGS

merry mishap

Postage goes green

I grew up in the 1950s and '60s, when postage was considerably cheaper and folks sent out a lot more Christmas cards. I remember helping my mother send out our cards.

The year I was 4, she signed the cards and addressed the envelopes, then let me lick them shut, carefully lick the stamps and stick them on the envelopes. When we ran out of postage stamps, my mother put the stack of unstamped cards on the table and went about her housework. I remembered that we had some stamps in one of the kitchen drawers, so I got them out and put them on the cards. Then I put the cards in with the others that were ready to be sent.

Days later, the postman came to our house carrying a handful of envelopes. I thought it was so exciting to get a whole bunch of cards to open and display in our house!

The mailman talked to my mom, and I was called to the door. That was when I learned the U.S. Post Office Department didn't take S&H Green Stamps.

—*Paulette Myers, Dubuque, Iowa*

a portable Christmas

By Dorothy Thomas, Homer, Louisiana

Christmas at our house has always been filled with special traditions, beginning with a trip to the country to find just the right tree. On Christmas Eve, my husband, Bill, would go out and buy additional presents for the family and for the employees at our tire store.

After church at 6 p.m., we went home for our traditional Christmas Eve feast—a bowl of Louisiana okra and shrimp gumbo. Then, at last, with festive Christmas music playing in the background, we opened our gifts.

Christmas Day was our time to relax together as a family. After a hearty late breakfast, we made eggnog for friends who dropped in during the afternoon. Anyone who was hungry was offered a do-it-yourself turkey sandwich.

In 1959, though, we weren't looking forward to Christmas. Bill had suffered a heart attack on Thanksgiving Day. He lived through it, but his progress wasn't good. In the hospital, he was quiet and seldom smiled.

The hospital was only two blocks from our home, so someone from the family was usually with him. But our efforts to cheer him up weren't working. Just before Christmas, our daughter, Mary, visited her dad and found tears rolling down his cheeks. "Oh, Daddy, what's wrong?" she asked.

"I want to be home for Christmas," Bill answered simply.

"Daddy, it doesn't matter where we are, just so we're together," she said.

"You mean you'll all be here?" Bill asked, brightening immediately.

"I promise," Mary assured him. After checking with his doctors, she rushed home to begin preparations. We sent son Billy to get a small tree for Bill's window. We gave him the decorations and gifts, and when he took them to Bill's room, he reported that Dad was smiling.

Then we went to work roasting a turkey, making gumbo and putting together the ingredients for eggnog. On Christmas Eve, when we arrived with hot gumbo, we found that Bill was very proud of himself. He'd asked a friend to do his shopping and had gifts for each of us. It was like old times, and it was so good to see Bill happy again.

On Christmas Day, we continued the family tradition with eggnog and turkey sandwiches in Bill's room. At 2 p.m., I put a sign on Bill's door: "Welcome. Come in. Have a cup of eggnog with us."

Old friends dropped in, as well as people we didn't know. Word spread through the hospital, and doctors, nurses and employees stopped by. "Oh, Mr. Thomas!" one nurse exclaimed. "You've brought Christmas to the hospital."

Bill was beaming. By 4, the eggnog was gone. After talking about his party for a while, Bill fell into a deep, contented sleep, the best medicine of all. It had been a great Christmas—and best of all, we had our Bill back. Mary was right: It doesn't matter where you are, as long as you're with those who love you.

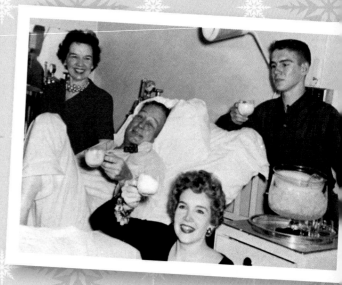

HOSPITAL HOLIDAY The Thomas family (from left, Dorothy, Bill, Mary and Billy) didn't let Bill's stay in the hospital halt their Christmas traditions.

Merry Christmas

TO ALL THE MILLIONS OF
"fresh up" families!

You like it...it likes you!

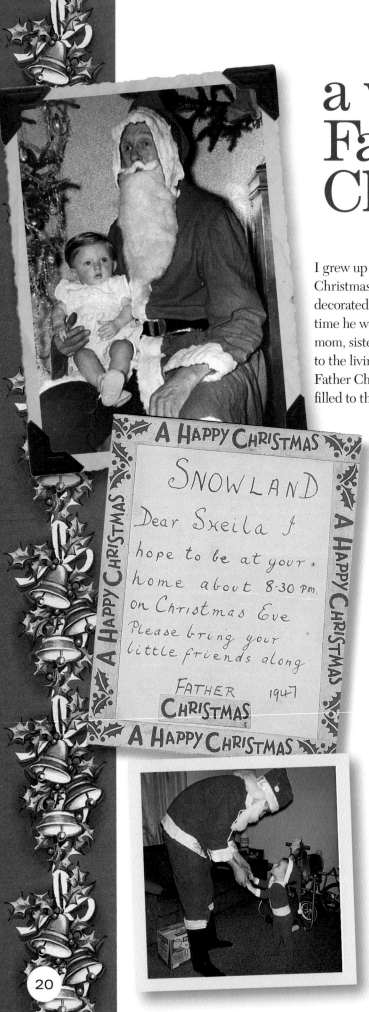

a visit from Father Christmas

By Sheila McCormick, Noblesville, Indiana

I grew up in the 1940s in Southport, England, where Father Christmas delivered our gifts from Snowland. I would get a decorated letter from Father Christmas each year telling me what time he would arrive on Christmas Eve. The family, including my mom, sister and aunts, along with my best friend, Rose, would go to the living room to wait for the doorbell to ring. In would come Father Christmas, ringing a big cowbell and carrying a huge sack filled to the top with goodies.

My dad, Charles Lloyd, was never in the room when Father Christmas arrived, because he needed to feed Father Christmas' reindeer. After Father Christmas left, Dad would reappear. Many years later, Rose and I confessed to each other that we'd known my dad was Father Christmas, but we didn't want to let on because we enjoyed the visits so much.

After opening our gifts, we would all have fruitcake and mince pie. At 11 o'clock, we would walk to church for candlelight services. We were up early on Christmas morning to prepare the dinner of turkey and all the trimmings, which we ate promptly at noon. Then Dad would pour brandy over the plum pudding and set it alight. It was lucky to find a charm in your pudding, and we ate carefully so as not to swallow one.

After dinner, we would all take a walk and then settle down for a snooze until the king's message came on the radio. In later years, we'd watch the queen on television.

I have been in the States for 49 years, and I have tried to make Christmas as magical for my children and grandchild as it was for me. That's why my late husband, Homer, always fed the reindeer when Father Christmas visited our house.

FATHERLY VISIT Sheila's dad was Father Christmas for his children and grandchildren, including grandson Raymond Clark in 1954 (top). Sheila still has her 1947 invitation (center), and she treasures this photo (left) of husband Homer McCormick with their son, Mark, in 1965.

straw for the cradle

By Peggie Kamm Bergantino, Northford, Connecticut

As our family grew in the 1950s and '60s, my husband, Mike, and I established some special Christmas traditions with our eight children to help them understand the meaning of the season.

At the beginning of Advent, each child received a small cradle to prepare for the Christ Child by earning straw bedding. Good deeds earned straw, while bad behavior meant that straw was taken away. Despite some cradles having a very thin layer of straw, each child found a baby Jesus on Christmas morning.

We also brought out an Advent calendar, a large piece of felt with a pocket for each day. Each pocket contained a task for each child to perform, such as writing a letter to Grandma or helping me with the baby.

On Christmas Eve, while Mike was still at work, I read the children a bedtime story that featured them as characters. When Mike got home about 10, all was quiet. So we went to work setting up and decorating the tree and retrieving the gifts we'd hidden.

We made many of the presents ourselves. Mike built doll cradles, toolboxes, banks and treasure chests. I made dolls and clothes. These heartfelt gifts and traditions always made Christmas special in our home.

HOMEMADE CRADLES Susan and Nancy Bergantino pose in front of the Christmas tree with the doll cradles their dad made in 1956.

my favorite childhood tradition

_____

_____

_____

_____

_____

_____

_____

a seat at the big table

By Bill Dumcum, St. Paul, Minnesota

We had many Christmas dinners with my mom's extended family, but the one I remember best was in 1954. I was 12 that year, and I got to sit at the big table—and what a big table it was!

We expected about 35 people, including my grandparents and five of my mom's seven siblings, for a Christmas meal at our house in Hugoton, Kansas. So we could all sit down together to eat, my dad set up sawhorses in the dining and living rooms and then placed boards on them to make a table that stretched across both rooms. We borrowed chairs from neighbors and set up card tables for the younger kids in the living room. There was room for everyone!

My mom oversaw the food preparation. My aunts took turns bringing and passing the food, while the men stayed mostly out of the way at the big table. Oh, how we ate, talked, laughed and just enjoyed being together.

After the tables had been cleared, my 17-year-old brother, Jack, got out his guitar, my grandfather uncased his fiddle, and a couple of my mom's sisters pulled out the piano bench. The piano players pounded out several variations of *Chopsticks*, and we all sang *You Are My Sunshine* at the top of our lungs.

My dad recorded the gathering on his old Sears, Roebuck reel-to-reel tape recorder. Right in the middle of all the singing, someone can be heard shouting, "Dennis, get off the table!" as my 11-year-old cousin tried to find a way to get over to the other side.

I'm so fortunate my dad made the recording. Being able to hear the singing, laughter and chatter from those relatives now gone is an absolute treasure.

FESTIVE FEAST
Grandparents, aunts, uncles and cousins assembled at a long table when Bill Dumcum's family hosted Christmas celebrations for his mother's extended family. About 35 people gathered to enjoy good food and good company.

warm glow of tree, family

By Nancy White, Omaha, Nebraska

I always loved Christmas Eve when I was growing up in Omaha in the 1940s and '50s. It was so full of joy and family traditions.

My dad would leave work about noon so he could pick up a tree at the lot down the street from our house. After Dad set the tree up in our living room, Mom would string the multicolored lights. As soon as she finished, my little brother, Kenny, and I would start hanging the ornaments and silvery icicles. We actually got along while we were decorating the tree!

The last thing to go on was the tinsel, which we threw on in clumps rather than placing it neatly and methodically. When we were finished, it was time to light our tree, which we thought was the most beautiful tree in the world.

When I was about 3, my dad made a little fireplace out of a big cardboard box, which he covered with brick-patterned paper. We put it up every Christmas and hung our stockings on it.

After a light supper, my mom would make popcorn balls and fudge while I did the dishes. Then we'd all gather around the tree and open presents from out-of-town family and friends. After that, Dad would settle into his comfortable chair to read us the Christmas story. That was the most important part of Christmas Eve, because it reminded us of the true meaning of Christmas. Then we'd sing our favorite carols and enjoy the special goodies that Mom had made.

Christmas Eve was such a happy time with my close and loving family. I've never wanted to change a single thing about our celebrations.

captured ~on~ cards

Family's annual photo greetings made lasting memories.

By Suzanne Manthe, Oak Creek, Wisconsin

Christmastime is always filled with anticipation, but it was especially so in our house, thanks to the special holiday cards made by our father, Charles Found.

Come December, our mother's pantry became Dad's photo studio. The sweet aroma of cookies and fruitcakes would mix with the scent of developing solutions.

Dad's interest in art and photography began when he was a student at the Wisconsin Lutheran Seminary and continued after his marriage to our mom, Ella, in 1942.

As the family grew in the '40s, '50s and '60s, so did the card productions, wherever we lived. After Dad had served a

congregation in Bristol, Wisconsin, we moved to Phoenix, Arizona, in 1956.

My favorite cards are from 1950 and 1952. I remember how excited we were in 1950 when we got to dress up in our Christmas outfits early (top left on facing page).

The 1952 card (top right on facing page) took us all to a friend's farm for a manger photo. We seemed so angelic as we gazed at Baby Jesus. In reality, the four of us could be a handful.

The 1954 card (bottom left on facing page), which features twins Bruce and Barbara looking into a store window, shows one of the elaborate sets Dad contrived. The window display was set up on our kitchen table. We painted Epsom salts on the windowpanes to make the frost.

Other photos included us singing, praying and baking Christmas cookies.

The tradition finally ended as the children left home and Dad's ministry took him to Africa for a time. But the fun memories of making those cards with Dad still enrich our lives today.

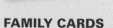

FAMILY CARDS
Charles Found came up with creative Christmas cards every year, as this display covering several decades shows.

MERRY CHRISTMAS

THE C. FOUNDS

"Kneel down and adore Him With Shepherds Tonight"
The C.E. Founds - 1952

"Bless all Thy dear children In Thy tender care." Amen.

The C. Founds 1960

Dad wasn't forgetful after all

By Sandi Schultz Hochburger, Marietta, Georgia

When I was growing up in Greendale, Wisconsin, in the 1940s, our family always walked to church for the Christmas Eve service. On the way, my dad would say, "I forgot to stoke the furnace. You go ahead, and I'll catch up with you at church."

Back home he would go, but not to stoke the furnace. Unbeknownst to me, he would get the gifts from the attic and put them under the tree.

Meanwhile, it was hard for me to keep my mind on church, because I just knew Santa soon would be delivering our presents. Sure enough, when we got home, all the gifts were under the tree! But before we could open them, I had to put on my pajamas and pose for a family picture taken by our neighbor.

Then my mom played Santa and handed out the gifts, which we opened one at a time. After that, we all enjoyed a big smorgasbord of sausage and cheese from Usinger's in Milwaukee.

Many Christmas Eves came and went before it dawned on me that my dad was probably not so forgetful after all.

SNEAKY DAD In 1948, pajama-clad Sandi (front) posed with her father, Gordon Schultz, mom Ethel, brothers, Wally and Larry, and Grandma Rupno.

Awe, Christmas tree!

When I was a child in the 1930s, the children, grandchildren and great-grandchildren of Albert and Anna Ekle gathered each Christmas Eve in the family home in Mankato, Minnesota. Mothers would gather to prepare the Norwegian *Julebord*—a spread of all kinds of good food—and then we'd attend church services.

After church, it was traditional for the entire family to line up by age, with the youngest child in front. While my aunt played the piano and we all sang *Silent Night*, the youngest would lead the way into the front sitting room, which was closed off by French doors.

You had to be 4 to lead the family. When my turn came, I felt so proud as my mother placed me at the head of the line. I led the family to the French doors, and as they were slid back into the wall, I saw the most beautiful Christmas tree, decorated in white with presents around it.

My mother told me I gave the loudest sigh of awe and stopped in the middle of the doors. I was so struck by the tree's beauty that I didn't move, preventing everyone else from moving, too. My embarrassed mother had to quickly step out of line and scoop me up so everyone could take their places around the tree.

—*Eugene Tate, Saskatoon, Saskatchewan*

merry mishap

CHRISTMAS

*Old as the spirit of giving . . .
new as a child's starry-
eyed wonder . . . Christmas
. . . world tradition! . . .
a tradition of man's faith
in things to come
. . . with its message
of universal brotherhood
. . . peace on earth . . .
good will to men.*

☆ ☆ ☆ ☆

Two Great American Traditions

FRUIT OF THE LOOM

REG. U. S. PAT. OFF.

Playing its part in this great tradition is the famous Fruit of the Loom label which appears on over 100 fine Cotton and Rayon Products. There's something for the whole family and the home in the Fruit of the Loom family . . . each backed by this guarantee of complete satisfaction.

the FRUIT of the LOOM guarantee

☆ ☆ ☆ ☆ ☆ If this Fruit of the Loom product does not give you satisfaction in use, return it to us and you will receive a new one or a refund of the purchase price. Fruit of the Loom, Inc., Providence, R. I.

FRUIT OF THE LOOM
*A family of American products
for the American family*

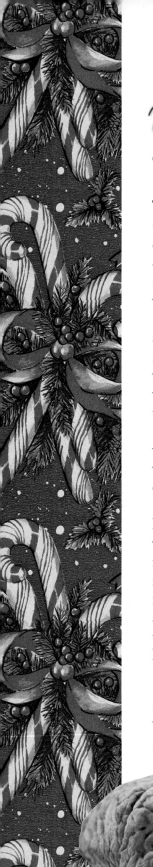

wrapped in tradition

These gift-giving traditions are fun and surprising additions to the holiday.

The great candy cane caper

One Christmas in the late '60s, someone in our family received a large candy cane, about 4 inches in diameter. What do you do with that much peppermint? In our family, the answer was: Have some fun!

The next Christmas, the candy cane appeared as a gift to another family member. From then on, every Christmas everyone would be looking for the candy cane, which was always cleverly wrapped to disguise its true identity.

One year, when our daughter and her family were with us for Christmas, my husband wrapped the candy cane in a big box and put our son-in-law's name on it.

Our son-in-law noticed that the candy cane had disappeared from storage and that there was a new gift under the tree for him. When no one was around, he opened the package, removed the candy cane and wrapped it up for my husband. Then he rewrapped the gift addressed to him and put it back under the tree. You can imagine the laughter when my husband opened his gift to find the candy cane.

—*Gloris Zoller, Pierre, South Dakota*

Dad had a gift for disguise

When I was growing up in the 1950s and '60s, my dad was always creative about wrapping gifts so we couldn't figure out what was in his packages.

One year I really wanted a transistor radio for Christmas. But my gift felt like a wastebasket. When I opened it, I found it was the wastebasket from my bedroom, complete with trash in it. When I dug through the trash, I found my radio.

In 1973, when I was expecting my first child and really needed money, my dad found a clever way to present it. A $50 bill was folded inside a walnut, quarters were placed under each piece of chocolate in a box of candy, and paper money was tucked among the pages of a paperback book.

I have carried on this family tradition with my sons, and now they delight in disguising everyone's Christmas gifts, too.

—*Kay Eitel, Angleton, Texas*

Stocking contains coal— and memories

In about 1940, when my brother and I were quite young, he opened a package to find a little stocking filled with coal. In those days, children were often warned that they had to be good or Santa would leave only coal in their stockings. The family laughed at the expression on my brother's face, but he received his share of toys, too.

After that, the stocking showed up every year, and everyone looked forward to seeing who would get it. We were all disappointed, but not surprised, when it disappeared one year. My mother had kept it from year to year, and she was getting forgetful.

The time came for her to move in with us. While helping clean out her apartment, I found a little box in the back of a drawer, and inside was the stocking! That Christmas, it was Mom's turn to receive the stocking.

Our family circle continues to grow, and the stocking, now a little unraveled and faded, appears every Christmas morning.

—*Eleene McNally Gallagher*
Richboro, Pennsylvania

sealed with a wish

"Remember when letters to Santa Claus were deposited in a little house like this in front of City Hall?" writes Margaret Rostedt of Montebello, California. "This photo was taken in White Plains, New York, in 1930 or '31. That's me mailing the letter as my brother and a friend attempt to peek into the house."

our family's funniest gift memory

good ol' days

This booklet was presented to me nearly 30 years ago after I admired it at my neighbor Lenore's house. At the time, Lenore told me she had received the booklet about 1940, and it had been a part of her Christmas ever since. It was a deluxe advertisement from some large company. She duplicated the pages for herself and tied them together with red yarn, then gave the original to me. It's been shared with others over the years, a sweet tradition that I intend to continue.

—*Christine Rauch*
Lake Villa, Illinois

all wound up

By Vicki Peihl, West Fargo, North Dakota

The best part of Christmas Eve when I was growing up wasn't the presents under the tree or all the delicious goodies. It was the old windup toys that Grandma brought out once a year.

There was a monkey that played cymbals and hopped around, a lumbering brown bear that growled and a rabbit with sharp metal teeth that nibbled a carrot. There were all kinds of fur-covered metal toys that made lots of noise. There were newer ones that ran on batteries, too, including a bear that poured coffee and drank out of the cup, a train that puffed smoke, a police car with a siren, and the newest and noisiest one of all, a rooster that crowed.

Each year, my siblings, cousins and I—13 of us in all—took the toys into the back room and tried to get them all wound up and going at once. The Mickey Mouse merry-go-round would spin its four riders, the police car would race around the floor, and the puppy dog would weave around our legs. We could never keep them all going at once, but it was fun to try!

The adults were gathered in the living room visiting and usually had to beg us to come open our gifts. The gifts were great! Grandma sewed clothing, doll clothes and stuffed animals and made decorated ornaments and bags; our uncle made wooden doll furniture; and our aunts always bought us games.

But as soon as we were done opening gifts, we headed back to the windup toys, for we knew they would soon be put away for another year.

my best grandparent memory

sweet small-town tradition

By Ben Romero, Fresno, California

When I was growing up in Nambe, New Mexico, Christmas morning was particularly sweet. Every year, any kid worth his salt would get up early and go around the neighborhood collecting candy, fruit and nuts.

The tradition was similar to trick-or-treating, except that we yelled, *"Mís Crismes!"* when the door opened. At houses where Anglo families lived, we exclaimed, "Merry Christmas!" before collecting our treats.

It wasn't the candy that made this tradition so special. It was sharing in the festive mood of every family in our small village. When the door opened, each house let out the wonderful aroma of baked goods, tamales, piñon wood and pine trees.

In 1960, when I was 8, it was particularly cold, with wet snow falling. I had been sick, and my mother was not going to let me go house to house. But when she could no longer stand the pitiful look on my face, she agreed to let me go with my 10-year-old brother, Louie, on one condition: I had to keep my head covered. I couldn't just wear a baseball cap, mind you. I had to wear a cloth diaper tied around my head like a scarf. I had to promise that I wouldn't take it off—and she reminded me that God was watching.

I kept looking around to make sure none of my friends saw me. Louie helped out, because he didn't want to be seen with me. At one house I waited near a tree while he went to the door, because I especially didn't want a certain girl to see me.

A few years later, we moved from Nambe to Española. We were not sure if the tradition was celebrated there, so my mom bought candy anyway. But nobody came. That's when we realized that our Christmas tradition was unique to the village of Nambe. It made me sad to know that my younger brothers would never partake in the experience, although at least they would be spared the humiliation of having to wear a diaper as they went door to door!

striped sisters

A striped pajama tradition that continues to this day began in 1959 for sisters Joanne, Suzi and Gerri Langguth of Ridley Park, Pennsylvania. The sisters dress up in holiday-striped pajamas every year when they join parents Larry and Jeannie for Christmas dinner.

family Nativity

The Cooke children of Reseda, California, portrayed the Nativity scene for many years for the family Christmas card. "Since we were blessed with another new baby every couple of years, we always had a little Christ Child," says mom JoAnn Schueller Cooke. "We mailed our last family Nativity scene in 1971, when Gina, the youngest, was 2½ and too big to portray a newborn babe." From left are Connie, Debbie, Kathy, Gina, Ted, Mark, Patrick and Mary.

CHAPTER TWO

Deck the Halls

It's hard to imagine anything more majestic than a Christmas tree adorned with dozens of heirloom ornaments and draped with glittering tinsel. It's one of many decorations—from the cherished plate that holds Santa's cookies to those personalized stockings in front of the fireplace—that make for lasting Christmas memories.

For Dorothy Burnette of Placentia, California, the decoration that most evokes the spirit of Christmas is a tabletop Santa lit by a lightbulb. Her parents, Mildred and Harold Hess of Los Angeles, bought the figurine in 1938 to celebrate her first Christmas.

"Every year, it's the first decoration to come down from the attic," Dorothy notes. "I keep it in a well-padded box. In my 71 years, I haven't celebrated a Christmas without it. As you can see by the photo (above right), the Santa still lights up after all these years and continues to give me and my family hours of pleasure during the holidays."

An angel is the most treasured decoration for Allen McMurphy of Richford, Vermont. "This tree-topper (right) was the first Christmas decoration my wife and I bought in 1946, the year we were married," he writes. "Last year was the 63rd consecutive year it adorned the top of our Christmas tree."

To read about more special decorations that light up the holidays, turn the page.

a tree for Mom

By Lyle Cate
Windsor Locks, Connecticut

During the Great Depression, Dad, Mom, my little brother, Jim, and I lived on a ranch in Wyoming, where my dad was the only full-time hired help. We lived in a small house with the bare minimum of conveniences about 20 miles from the nearest town. One of my chores was to chop wood for heating and cooking.

My mother was a quiet woman, not in the least demanding or discontented with her life. It was something of a surprise when she said to me one day in early December when I was 11, "It would be so nice if we could have a Christmas tree this year."

She knew, of course, that we couldn't afford a tree. Anyway, the closest place to buy one would probably be in Cheyenne, some 100 miles away, and there was no such thing as an artificial tree then. As for the old-fashioned custom of going into the woods and finding a tree, good luck! Scrub pines were the rule, and I mean scrub.

Still, I told her, "I don't remember seeing any in the hills, but I'll go out Saturday and see if I can find something."

Saturday was a nice clear day, maybe 10 to 15 degrees above zero. I left about 8 a.m., after finishing my chores, to search for the perfect tree. The hills in back of the ranch were the very smallest foothills of the Rocky Mountains but seemed mighty high as I climbed them. I tramped for hours, and my standards for the perfect tree grew less demanding as the day wore on. It must have been about 2:30 when I decided to give up. While thinking of my mother's disappointment, I rounded a rock—and there was a beautiful 6-foot fir tree.

Don't tell me there isn't a God looking after poor little kids in Wyoming. I couldn't believe my good fortune, and I almost cried thinking of how happy my mother would be. I quickly chopped down this miracle and headed for home.

I left the tree outside and tried to put on a sad face to fool Mom. "I didn't find the right tree for us, Mom," I told her, "but I found something that we might be able to use." I couldn't contain myself for long, however, as I was bursting to show it to her. When she looked at it, I saw the tears she tried to hide, and I knew she was happy.

There was never a Christmas tree that was more admired than that little one adorned with strings of popcorn and construction-paper chains, with a shiny star saved from more prosperous times on top. The gifts, mostly the result of Mom's ability to make much of little, were all our family needed to feel like the luckiest people in the world.

TREE OR NO TREE Lyle Cate, pictured with his father, James, in 1939, recalls that his family had faith in God, love for one another and confidence in a better tomorrow.

Deck the Halls

a string of popcorn

For newlyweds, homespun decoration beckoned an uninvited guest.

By Millie DesEnfants, Shelbyville, Indiana

In early December 1944, I was a new bride. John and I wanted to be together every minute before he went overseas, so we married sooner than we'd planned and drove to Greenfield, near Indianapolis. John would have to report to Camp Atterbury in a few days. Our apartment was the cheapest we could find, and the furniture was sparse. But we were so in love that it didn't matter. After we'd bought groceries and settled in, John seemed to read my mind when he said, "OK, let's go find a Christmas tree!" We looked hard and finally found a tree that was small enough to fit on a little table in front of our living room's only window.

The next morning we held hands and caught snowflakes on our tongues as we headed to the Ben Franklin store around the corner. We spent all the nickels and dimes we could spare on a few glass ornaments, a strand of lights and some icicles for the tree. I wanted to surprise John, so I didn't tell him why I'd bought a package of sewing needles and a spool of thread. I had already snuck a sack of popcorn into our groceries.

After we arrived at our little love nest, we decorated the tree and were so pleased. Then I showed John how to shake the skillet while the corn popped. I threaded some needles and we sat on the bed and strung the popcorn. It was the final decoration for the finest tree in Greenfield, Indiana.

The third day arrived, and that was a sad one: John would have to report to camp. He headed out with his duffel bag to warm up the car, promising to come back to say goodbye. I stood alone, looking at the door that had closed behind him, and felt the tears rolling down my cheeks. I turned around to admire our Christmas tree—so beautiful.

And then I saw the branches move. I thought the wind might be coming through a broken windowpane—until I reached into the tree and saw the two beady eyes of the mouse that was eating our popcorn. I always have been scared to death of mice, and I screamed just as John walked in the door. After calming me down, he made a quick trip to the dime store for a mousetrap.

We have laughed through the years about our guest that first Christmas together. We have also given thanks that John was one of the lucky servicemen to come home from the war.

The next Christmas we were together, I wondered what was in the small box under the tree. This time, laughter filled the room as I opened John's surprise. It was a mousetrap!

TEMPTING TREE Millie DesEnfants, shown here at 19, didn't expect her homespun garland to appeal to anyone but her new husband, John.

model memories

By David Neimeyer, Fogelsville, Pennsylvania

Growing up in the 1950s and '60s, I loved adding to our model train layout each Christmas. My father would set up two sawhorses with plywood. The plywood was painted green, with a gray oval painted near the edge to simulate a highway. Some years, we set up our Christmas tree on top of the platform. This made for a challenge when cars jumped the track behind the tree. Occasionally, a strand of tinsel would fall across the track, shorting out the train.

We had three trains, all OS gauge. Two were from the late 1930s. One had been my father's, the other my uncle's. Each had five cars: a locomotive; a black coal tender; a low, black, open gondola car; an orange boxcar with the Baby Ruth logo on its side; and a red caboose. We bought the third train, a red-and- silver diesel locomotive with several cars, around 1960.

We delighted in finding ways to arrange the track for the best display. We had a number of classic Plasticville houses for the layout. There were two colonial-style farmhouses, a small cottage (which we sometimes used as a template for gingerbread houses), a school, a church, a firehouse and a farm. For me, however, the highlights were always the signs my father made proclaiming "Welcome to Dianeville, Pop. 1" (for my older sister), and another for me that read "Davidtown."

The train platform now sits unused along the back wall of the garage. The trains and houses have been parceled out to grandsons. However, on a model train layout in my basement, a small green and white sign still beckons with its cheerful "Welcome to Davidtown."

TREASURED TRACKS
The "Davidtown" sign (above left) was a fixture every Christmas when David Neimeyer and his dad and sister set up their model train layout.

no mistletoe in sight

Sisters Susan and Pam Lichty may have seen Mommy kissing Santa Claus, but Bob Lichty saw his daughters kissing each other and couldn't resist snapping their picture in 1954 in Texas. The coffee table was just the right height for the girls to get into the spirit of the season as they admired some festive decorations. Bob now lives in Vacaville, California.

the story behind our tree topper

our magical pinecone

By Paul Lacourse
Manchester, New Hampshire

My fondest Christmas memory was in the early '50s when I was about 5 years old and my little sister was almost 2. My father, who loved Christmas, decided that we would go out to look for a magical Christmas cone and plant our own Christmas tree. So one Sunday, my parents took us out to the state park and told us to look for the perfect pinecone. I showed a couple of prospects to my father, but he rejected each one, saying it was not special enough.

Eventually I found one that met my father's approval, and we headed home to plant it. My sister and I decorated a terra-cotta flowerpot with festive Christmas colors and glitter, then my father planted the pinecone in soil and put the flowerpot into a large tin washbasin in the front parlor. He said it was our job to water the cone each day.

Unbeknownst to us, after about a week, my father switched the cone for a pine branch. Every few days he would replace the branch with a larger one.

On Christmas Eve, we went to bed early, because Santa would be coming and would decorate our magic tree for us. Christmas morning my parents woke us up with a twinkle in their eyes. They said that Santa had indeed come during the night, and our little branch had turned into a majestic Christmas tree.

When my sister and I looked, we found a real miracle that Christmas morning: an 8-foot tree beautifully decorated with colored lights, angel hair and glass balls.

This was a Christmas that has never left my mind. I am now in my 60s and I have tried over the years to be like my dad and give my children and grandchildren loving memories to cherish forever.

PROUD OF PINECONE
Paul Lacourse and his sister, Terri, are shown here with their cousin and her husband in front of a family Christmas tree like the one they "grew" from a pinecone.

merry
mishap

Precious, but not picturesque

One year, during the Great Depression and the Dust Bowl in eastern Colorado, my oldest brother, Ray, who was working in Boulder, brought home a real tree for Christmas. It was only about 15 inches tall, but to my sister, Mary Jean, and me, it was a real treat. (In the past, a small tumbleweed had served as our tree.)

Mary Jean and I loved our real tree. We made decorations with English walnut shells we glued together and colored with crayons. After Christmas, we just couldn't throw the tree out, because we might not have another one. So we put it in a box in the attic to save for next year. The next year, when we got the box out, we were disappointed to find that all the needles had dried up and fallen off. Still, we used the tree for another year or two. It may not have been the grandest tree ever, but it was the one we both remember.

— *Weldon Neuschwanger, Olympia, Washington*

special town, special gifts

I was born in Ottawa, Kansas, and grew up knowing the wonderful people who were merchants in town. On this Christmas—1949 or 1950—I recall receiving two special gifts. One was a wreath from the pharmacist who ran the drugstore on North Main Street. To me, the bright-red wreath with a light was the very symbol of Christmas. Every holiday season, I placed it in a front window so everyone driving by our farm could see it. The other gift, shown on the arm of the chair behind me, was a black rabbit from Fivian's feed store. Looking back, I realize how lucky I was to have lived in a time when such items could mean so much.

— *Donald Hawley*
Lawrence, Kansas

baby brother's
big beautiful tree

By Nancy Case, Alva, Oklahoma

Christmas 1953 was special for my sister and me because it was the first one for our new baby brother. Peggy, 10, and I, 11, couldn't wait for the many exciting, new things Johnny was to discover.

We lived on a farm near Cora in northwest Oklahoma, and choosing a tree that year was especially important. We went with our dad to the pasture and finally picked out the most beautiful tree. We watched Daddy cut it down and place it in the back of the pickup; we took such care hanging the ornaments and lights. I'm not sure that Johnny, at 6 months old, appreciated all the beauty, but Peggy and I did.

Watching our baby brother with his gifts on Christmas Eve was special. This was probably the first Christmas that my sister and I thought more about giving than receiving. After everything was opened, Daddy took pictures with his new camera, the first we ever had with an indoor flash. After each picture was taken we saw big blue spots for several minutes. Even so, Peggy and I thought it was a perfect Christmas.

Several years ago, we were recalling what a pretty Christmas tree we had the year Johnny was born, and my daughter, Natalie, asked if we had any pictures. When I located the famous snapshots, my jaw dropped. The tree wasn't nearly as large as I remembered. I showed it to Peggy and we both exclaimed, "This is a Charlie Brown tree!"

TREE LOOMS LARGE
The family Christmas tree was smaller and sparser than Peggy Barnes Mapes (left) and author Nancy Barnes Case, holding their brother, Johnny, remembered. But their smiles were big and full.

heavenly view

Maggie Thomas wore a festive corsage and some sparkly trim when she struck a glamorous pose next to her equally glamorous Christmas tree in Elyria, Ohio, in 1962. She recalls that she had just renovated her apartment, which had 12-foot ceilings. "I found a 12-foot tree in the lot at Sears downtown. The salesman was kind enough to deliver the tree up 15 flights of stairs," says Maggie, who now lives in Lakeshore, Florida. "As you can see, it was in the days of angel hair!"

memories of my childhood Christmas tree

_____

_____

_____

_____

_____

_____

_____

homes dressed in their holiday best

For many *Reminisce* readers, decorating their houses for the season is a fun way to get into the Christmas spirit.

Shiny and new

When aluminum trees became popular, Lewis and Dorothy Wilhelm bought a beautiful one. "Here is Uncle Lewis and Aunt Dot's tree in December 1962, surrounded by decorations and gaily wrapped packages," writes Mary Ann Gove of Cottonwood, Arizona.

Festive fake fireplace

For houses without a fireplace, the next best thing was a cardboard version hung with stockings, like this one in the home of Pearl Blair in Superior, Wisconsin. Granddaughters Jodi and Cindy Korpela were photographed during a 1965 visit to Grandma Pearl. Jodi, 4, "looks delighted holding the puppy," which was not a Christmas present, says their mom, Janice Korpela of Cornucopia, Wisconsin. "I have no idea who owned the puppy."

Colorful card collection

Christmas cards remain a festive way to decorate, whether displayed on mantels and tabletops or hung in archways and along staircases. In 1956, when Frances Kocman Sabo was a little girl in Hammond, Indiana, the seasonal greetings covered a door with their vibrant colors.

"The anticipation of Christmas at the Kocman house was magical," she says. "It was such a wonderful time to be a child."

Beautiful bubble lights

Bubble lights were all the rage in the late 1940s and 1950s. "This bubble light tree is among our most cherished Christmas decorations," writes Carolyn von Gohren of Olympia, Washington. "My paternal grandfather, Samuel Ashby, gave it to my parents and me in the early 1950s. He sent it to us from the Paris Company, a Salt Lake City department store for which he had been a buyer. The 27-inch tree has 18 lights that 'bubble' once their liquid reaches a certain temperature. In our family home in Seattle, the tree was placed in the living room bay window."

Stairway of stockings

Children can't resist Christmas stockings, and adults, if they're honest, will admit a sentimental fondness for them, too. The Bennett siblings of Crystal, Minnesota, ranged in age from 4 to 12 in 1957 when they lined up with stockings embroidered by their grandma. From left are Jeanne Bennett Dwyer, Kathy Bennett Beatty, Donna Bennett Dowd, Barb Bennett Burchill and Lee Bennett.

festive flocked tree

This photo of my sister, Marilyn, 8, behind me was taken in 1946 when I was 6 and got this new tricycle for Christmas. We lived in Oakland, California, at the time. Our dad, Richard Merrill, was a commercial artist, so he would create things like these candy canes with the cellophane ribbons. He would do the flocked trees for us, too, always finding ways to make our holidays special.

— *Jay Finlay, Phoenix, Arizona*

Have a Pepsi, merry people!

EVEN IN THIS SEASON of tradition, you'll notice some new trends—
in the way that people look and feel.

Lighter, less-filling food and drink help today's moderns celebrate merrily—but stay slim.
That's why today's Pepsi-Cola, reduced in calories, is especially welcome at today's
festive occasions. Never heavy, never too sweet, it refreshes without filling.
Have plenty of Pepsi on hand for the holidays!

The Light refreshment

circa 1950

tree-decorating tradition

By Peggy Edinger Bodenburg, Elk Mound, Wisconsin

Most people had their trees in their picture windows weeks before Christmas when I was a child in the 1950s and '60s in northern Wisconsin. But my family waited until Christmas Eve, a tradition passed down from my dad's side of the family.

Once the supper table was cleared, the wait was finally over. Dad would bring in the tree with cross boards nailed to its trunk. If there was a big gap between the branches, he would use his hand drill to make a hole where he could attach extra greenery. By the time he'd finished getting the tree ready, my seven siblings and I would have brought all the decorations from the crawl space. The boxes were always cold, but when we opened them the beautiful ornaments filled the room with a rich radiance.

My older siblings would put the strings of lights on the tree. Some of the lights had reflectors around them, and a few had special bulbs that blinked and twinkled. Next came the strands of glass beads, and only after that could we younger kids start hanging all the colorful glass balls. One special decoration was a Santa made out of cotton batting that had been our great-grandma's.

Finally, with all the ornaments hung, it was time for the tinsel, which was saved from year to year. We younger ones were not allowed to hang those fragile metallic strands.

By this time it was well past my bedtime. I would kneel at the side of my bed to say my prayers, including a plea for a toy I desperately wanted. Then I would jump into bed and nestle down under the feather tick, visions of Santa and our magical tree filling my every thought.

THROUGH THE YEARS Peggy Edinger was 7 in 1960 when she showed off her new doll near the Christmas tree (left). With her are brothers Gary and Jerry and their dog, Patsy. Peggy's parents, Jess and Albina Edinger (center), enjoy their tree on Christmas in the early '60s. Peggy was 17 in 1970 when she and future husband Gary Bodenburg posed (right) with nephew Thad.

front yard fa-la-la-la-la

Handmade projects were the hallmark of the Christmas displays in Paul L. Prough Jr.'s yard in Mount Union, Pennsylvania, during the 1950s. "Starting around Labor Day, my father, Paul Sr., and my mother, Polly, could be found in the basement drawing, hammering, sawing and painting. Their projects required long hours, hard work and a little patience, but they did bring happiness to others," he writes. Here Paul Jr. and his mother sing along with three carolers near the lamppost in the family's front yard.

CHAPTER THREE

Acts of Faith

Advent wreaths, Nativity scenes, church services and other sacred traditions are central to the holiday for many families. For Kristi Quigley of Rockford, Illinois, childhood in the 1960s included memorable Christmas morning services.

"Our family of five would make the six-hour drive to our grandparents' home, arriving late on Christmas Eve," she recalls. "Christmas morning brought the bustle of eating breakfast, getting ready for church and enjoying just being together again. We would arrive for Mass to find the church beautifully decorated with flickering white lights and the Nativity on the altar. We'd sing Christmas carols, feeling the wondrous miracle of the holiday."

The Sudiks of Wahoo, Nebraska, never missed midnight Mass on Christmas Eve in the 1950s.

"My mom would fix up my hair in pin curls and do the same for my sisters," recalls Mary Beth Fulton of Lincoln. "We'd wear new dresses with black patent-leather shoes and carry matching purses.

"After a traditional fish dinner, Dad would ask me and my siblings—Judy, Janice and Terry—to kneel in front of our Christmas tree and say a prayer (above right). Then we'd go to St. Wenceslaus Catholic Church, where there'd be folding chairs in the aisle to handle the overflow crowd."

For more stories about the devotional traditions of Christmas, read on.

the sneak peek

By Don Doyle, Lansdowne, Pennsylvania

When I was growing up, bedtime on Christmas Eve was very, very early. We never minded, though, because we reasoned that the sooner we fell asleep, the sooner it would be Christmas morning.

But this year, 1955, would be different, because, along with my older brothers, I had been chosen to be an altar boy for midnight Mass. I would dress in a cassock and surplice and assist the priests. I had to be at the church by 10:30 p.m.

I had big plans for this night. I knew my mother would wake us about 10 p.m. to get dressed and walk the four blocks to church. In my mind, Santa would already have stopped at my house by that time. That meant the tree would be beautifully decorated and the presents placed around the living room. As I came down the steps I would get a sneak peek at what wonderful things were in store for me in the morning!

It never occurred to me to ask my older brothers, Jeff and Dick, about it. They had done the midnight Mass routine for several years. Why had they never mentioned this great opportunity to me? Maybe they were sworn to secrecy—but now I would be in on the secret.

When the big night came, my mother entered our room and quietly woke Jeff, Dick and me, being careful not to disturb our younger brothers, Mark and Bobby. We dressed in our Sunday suits with white shirts and ties. I confess that I didn't see the sense in this, because we'd be entirely covered by our liturgical garb, but I didn't protest. I had other things on my mind.

I was the first one ready. I walked to the stairs, but no sooner did I extend one foot than my mother commanded me: "Stop right where you are!" I protested, "Mom, I can't be late," but it did no good.

To my horror, Mom reached into her apron pocket, withdrew a cotton

ZIPPED LIPS The Doyle children, gathered for a Christmas photo in 1954 (top), are Bob (foreground) and (from left) Mark, author Don, Dick, Jeff and Kathryn Adelaide with Dave on her lap. Dressed for midnight Mass that year (center) are altar boys Jeff (left) and Dick, the big brothers who didn't spill the beans. On Christmas Day, Don shows off his new rifle (bottom) as Dick (left), Jeff, mom Kitty and dad Art look on.

handkerchief and fastened it over my eyes as if I were about to face a firing squad.

As I was led down the stairs, I was incredulous. I had planned this night since October! Every night I envisioned how wonderful it would be to get just a little peek at Santa's handiwork on Christmas Eve.

The door opened and cold December air assaulted me. On the porch the handkerchief was removed, and I was given my instructions: Stay with your brothers, meet your grandmother, and everyone walk home together. "Yes, Mother," was all I could say.

Midnight Mass was a solemn high Mass, a very long Mass, but my mind was not on the service. I was formulating a new plan.

All was not lost, I reasoned. I had one more chance to make my dream come true. The front porch of our house had a large window with a venetian blind that was always open. I would start running when we reached the corner, sprint up the steps and gaze into the living room.

After Mass, Grandmother Farren was waiting for us in the schoolyard, and we

My mother had two sisters but no brothers. How did it happen that she knew all about boys? I don't know. I'll never know. One thing I do know: She had eyes in the back of her head.

started the walk home. When we finally reached the corner of our street, I began my sprint, as planned.

I passed the vacant lot, and then the five houses that came before ours. Triumphantly, I bounded up the 11 steps to the porch and raced to the window—only to find the blinds drawn.

I couldn't believe it. They were never closed. Never, except tonight.

In a moment, my grandmother and brothers arrived. Both Jeff and Dick had strangely knowing looks on their faces. No one said a word. Then it dawned on me: This must be the way it always plays out. It happened to Jeff, and then to Dick, exactly the same way. Now it was my turn.

Every two years the same scene would unfold. A rite of passage for an 8-year-old boy who thinks he knows it all.

My mother had two sisters but no brothers. How did it happen that she knew all about boys? What made her so smart? I don't know. I'll never know. One thing I do know: She had eyes in the back of her head.

Oh, by the way, I never told Mark about that Christmas Eve. Or Bob. Or Dave.

my favorite Christmas hymn

_____

_____

_____

_____

more in the manger

The Siebert family of rural Avon, New York, sent this homemade manger scene as their 1954 Christmas card. Standing, from left, are Dan, 10; Ron, 12; and Joanne, 4. The babies are twins Paul and Gary, just a month old. "It was a perfect scene for a very memorable Christmas for our growing family," writes their mother, Dolores, who now lives in Saratoga, California.

silent night

By Geri Frost Stratman, Omaha, Nebraska

In 1947, as a senior at Holy Name High School in Omaha, I helped the Rev. Joseph Campbell teach catechism to Catholic students from the nearby school for the deaf.

Eight-year-old Jimmy was in our class. Shortly before Christmas, in eager sign language, he told me about the truck he wanted from Santa—a red-and-white one with rubber wheels. But Father Campbell, who saw our conversation, knew that unless we bought the truck, Jimmy wouldn't get it. Money was scarce at his house; Jimmy's daddy no longer lived there.

Christmas Eve morning, Father Campbell gave me $5 to buy presents for Jimmy's family. Then he filled a basket with food and topped it with candy canes.

That evening, Father Campbell, my friend Ray and I drove to Jimmy's house. Jimmy came to the door. His deaf mother, with a small child in her arms and a toddler clinging to her, stood next to him. Except for a flickering candle, the house was dark—the electricity had been shut off.

Father went next door to call the utility company and promise that he'd make good on the bill if they turned the power back on. Ray and I drove to a nearby market to buy a marked-down tree, a string of lights and a few ornaments.

When we returned to Jimmy's house, the lamp in the living room burned brightly. We brought in the gifts. I handed a doll to the toddler, who cradled it in her arms and murmured, "Baby, baby." Jimmy's older brother got checkers, and there was a pull toy for the baby. When Jimmy saw his truck, he started to jump up and down. No words were necessary.

I'd never cried on Christmas Eve before, but I wasn't alone. When Father gave Jimmy's mother the groceries, tears ran down her cheeks. Before we left, we put up the Christmas tree and helped the kids decorate it.

I knew I'd never forget that evening or the happy faces of Jimmy's joyful family.

Silent night, holy night
All is calm, all is bright
Round yon Virgin
Mother and Child
Holy Infant so tender
and mild
Sleep in heavenly peace
Sleep in heavenly peace

Silent Night was a poem written in 1816 by an Austrian priest named Joseph Mohr. It is the most famous Christmas carol of all time.

Acts of Faith

stitched with prayers

By Josephine Schulte, San Antonio, Texas

In our German-American home in the '30s, it was the custom to suspend an Advent wreath—in German, *Adventskranz*—from the ceiling of our living room. The circle of evergreen branches, we children learned, symbolized the endless nature of God's love.

Four candles in makeshift holders adorned the wreath. Each of the four Sundays before Christmas, another candle was lit, and we four kids always argued about whose turn it was to have this very special privilege.

In our household, family devotions were held in the form of a daily rosary. During Advent, to make praying more interesting for us kids, Mama would say, "Now we are going to knit the cap, sweater and booties for the Baby Jesus, but we have to hurry so everything will be ready when he arrives."

Each prayer symbolized a certain number of stitches, and Mama kept us informed each day of how far we'd advanced. "Now we've finished one sleeve on the sweater," she'd tell us. "We'll start the second sleeve tomorrow."

It helped keep us kids excited about the arrival of the Christ Child. And when Christmas finally came, his baby clothes, stitched with our prayers, were ready to wear.

ADVENT TRADITION Prayers took on a special significance in the days before Christmas for Josephine Schulte, seated second from left (below) in 1932 at age 3 and standing with bike (left) in 1941 at age 12.

spirit shines brightly

By Harold Gerbers, Fort Wayne, Indiana

Before 1952, it seemed as though Santa and the reindeer won the major Christmas lighting awards in Fort Wayne, Indiana. For a place known as a city of churches, this did not seem right. So my wife and I decided to do our part to change this picture.

In 1953, months before Christmas, we started planning our outdoor decorating and light displays. We chose the theme "Glory to God." It took the rest of the year to make and paint the cutouts for the host of angels on our roof. We were so very pleased to have this display receive the first-place award that year.

Over the years, we featured other themes, including "Prince of Peace," "Let us Adore Him," "Happy Birthday," "Christmas Blessings" and "Jesus Christ is Born Today." Other awards followed, but more important, there were soon many other displays depicting the true meaning of Christmas.

In 1959, our two boys, Joel Allen, who was 9, and Thomas David, who was 5, looked forward to the display because they were pictured in life-size color cutouts. It took years for us to complete the entire Nativity picture, but we finally displayed it in our yard and the one next door, where my wife's mother lived.

Our Christmas displays were popular for many years, drawing onlookers even after the lighting contests ended. The Christmas story and carols played over our loudspeaker proclaimed the joy of the Savior's birth to people of all faiths, many of whom would stop by to express their appreciation.

Not only was the planning and decorating a lot of fun for our family, but the joy was multiplied when we saw hundreds of others finding the spirit of Christmas through our efforts.

AWARD WINNERS Year after year during the 1950s, outdoor displays that depicted the true meaning of Christmas garnered awards and visitors at the Harold Gerbers family home in Fort Wayne, Indiana.

triumphant task

By Walter Dzik, St. Petersburg, Florida

The first Christmas Eve I remember was in 1931 or '32, when I was a boy in Donora, Pennsylvania. That was the year my mom sent me out into the snow-covered foothills nearby on a very important mission: to gather dried grass for the centerpiece of our table.

Placed under the plate that would hold the holy bread and flanked by two candles, the grass was the most important thing on the table, Mom said, because it represented the straw in the manger on which the Christ Child lay.

I was very honored by my mom's request, but also a little anxious, because she told me that we needed grass that had never been walked on. How would I find such a thing?

I remember walking the path the children took to go to school. I dared not brush away the snow and pick my grass from there, because how could I be sure no one had stepped on it?

Then I tried a steep hill with many ditches where the water ran off. That's when I saw it: a big clump of dry grass hanging over the side of a deep ditch. Surely no one could have walked on this grass without falling face-first into the ditch.

Carefully, I got down on my belly about a yard away from my prize and, using my elbows, inched my way toward the overhanging grass. When it was in reach, I pulled a fistful and stuffed it into my coat.

I hurried home with my precious cargo close to my heart. I felt warm and at peace, and my mother was full of love and praise for my accomplishment. That same warmth returns each time I remember that Christmas.

noel, noel

"My sister, now Peggy Phillips-Keeble (left), was 8 and I was 10 when this picture was taken in our living room in Corpus Christi, Texas, in 1943," writes Ann Staton-Keeble, who still lives in Corpus Christi. The girls, who frequently sang at church, were practicing for its Christmas program. At the piano is their aunt Anna Belle Allen.

Her tiny voice was heard

In 1929 when I was 3 years old, I was to be in the annual Christmas Eve program at the little country church that my family attended in Edgewood, Iowa.

Every time I rehearsed my lines at home, my mother would say, "Now speak nice and loud so Ben Wessel (our next-door neighbor who was hard of hearing) can hear you."

On Christmas Eve, when it was my turn to speak at the program, I just barely got on stage and meekly recited, "I'm just a little girl, but I can say to you, I wish you a merry Christmas, I really truly do."

Then, at the top of my lungs, I yelled, "Did you hear that, Ben Wekkle?"

The little church, packed to the balcony, just roared with laughter. My mother was so embarrassed that I became embarrassed, too.   —*Joyce Appleton Jackson, Sarasota, Florida*

merry mishap

blizzard broadcast

By the Rev. Charles Fair, Wyomissing, Pennsylvania

It was Saturday, Christmas Eve, 1966. The snow kept falling faster and heavier in our part of Pennsylvania, and many pastors and priests were canceling services because of the blizzard. But our church, Alsace Lutheran in Reading, had a blessing others did not. We broadcast regular radio services each Sunday, and canceling this weekend would mean canceling not only our Christmas Day program but the special one we had planned for Christmas Eve. As pastor, I was determined to make it over the snowdrifts so we could broadcast both services.

I decided to head out Saturday afternoon and sleep at the church so I didn't miss the Christmas Day service. My wife, Louise, who had been my partner in ministry for many years, announced that she and our children—then ages 9, 7 and 1½—were coming along.

Quickly, we collected blankets, pajamas, warm clothing, sermon notes and the Christmas turkey, jammed them in the car and then inched along the three miles of unplowed streets to the church. The organist and the choristers were snowed in, but our sexton and radio operator had managed to make it. As we hastily made sleeping arrangements on sofas and cots, Louise prepared a turkey dinner.

With most churches snowed in, our radio audience would be large. But without the organist or choir, what would we do about music? Louise said she would play the piano, and she quickly arranged a duet for our older son and daughter to sing. I can still hear the sounds of their voices singing out: "Ring the bells, let the whole world know, Christ is born in Bethlehem."

Despite the blizzard, more than 100 people made it to church to worship with us, and thousands listened by radio. We went on the air at 11 p.m. and ended at midnight with *Silent Night*. Then, after bedding down for the night, we woke early Sunday morning to broadcast the Christmas message to great numbers of snowbound listeners.

But there was one more challenge. Santa hadn't visited our church that night; how would he get to our house? Louise came to the rescue again: If she could get home before the children and me, she said, she could be Santa's helper. A generous church member quickly took her home, and she finished up all of the holiday preparations.

It was truly a Christmas to remember. We managed to broadcast two live services during a blizzard— and, yes, Santa got to our house in time to surprise our three children.

SNOWED IN The Rev. Charles Fair and his family (far left), including 1½-year-old Jonathan, prepare for bed after broadcasting Christmas Eve services, which featured wife Louise, son Daniel, and daughter Rebecca (left).

PART OF THE AMERICAN SCENE

White Christmas

"Toward Evening," a twilight snowscape by Ernest Fiene, whose paintings hang in the Metropolitan Museum, the Art Institute of Chicago, the Detroit Art Institute, and other collections.

and it's Maxwell House wherever you go—

Snow for Christmas—perennial hope for the holidays! Snow to waken the sleighbells . . . to wrap the houses in festive white . . . to embroider the trees with beauty. Part of our Christmas tradition—part of our American Scene.

And indoors, by the festive Christmas fireside, Maxwell House too is part of the American scene, for it is America's favorite coffee. Today Maxwell House is enjoyed by *more* people than any other

brand of coffee in America for its rich, *extra* flavor!

Many choice Latin-American coffees are blended by experts to give Maxwell House that satisfying *mellowness . . . vigor . . . richness . . . full body*. Then "Radiant Roasting" develops the *full* flavor goodness. That's why, North, South, East, or West, it's Maxwell House wherever you go!

Tune in . . . Maxwell House Coffee Time . . . starring George Burns and Gracie Allen, NBC, Thursday night.

MAXWELL HOUSE, TOO, IS PART OF THE AMERICAN SCENE

Good to the Last Drop!

No wonder it's bought and enjoyed by more people than any other brand of coffee in America!

A Product of General Foods

stars in her eyes

By Doreen Irving, Medicine Hat, Alberta

In 1940, when I was 3, my family moved to tiny Hatton, Saskatchewan, where there was no running water or electricity. There was, however, a beautiful white church with a stately steeple.

On Christmas Eve, we went to church—and what a magical sight awaited inside! Boughs of aromatic pine adorned the stage and formed a framework for the organ and organist. Streamers of red, white and green made a wonderful design in the rafters.

Several pews had been removed to make room for a magnificent Christmas tree, so tall that I had to look way up to see the star on top. It was round and full and smelled as if it had just come from the forest. I loved the garlands of popcorn and cranberries and the lovely ornaments, but best of all were the dozens and dozens of candles in holders.

When all the candles were lit, the ornaments glimmered and glowed as if a fairy had waved her wand over them.

What a sight for a 3-year-old who had never seen a Christmas tree before!

The choir and congregation sang lovely Christmas carols, their voices blending in beautiful harmony. When they sang *Silent Night*, I felt goose bumps run all the way up my arms.

The pastor told the story of the birth of Baby Jesus, and then the elders came up to the front to pass out bags of candy and nuts to all the children—even me! The brown paper bag felt rough in my hands, but it held such tasty treats: rainbow-colored hard candy, sugary pastel rosebuds and creamy chocolates of every kind; a variety of nuts, an apple and an orange. What a treasure! I savored it all long after Christmas Eve.

We walked home in the moonlight with millions of stars twinkling in the sky and no streetlights or neon signs to compete with them. But to me, even the stars in the sky couldn't outshine that sparkling, magical Christmas tree.

Mom's precious keepsake

By Dianne Murray, Ridgecrest, California

In the early '60s in our Mojave Desert town in California, my mom and I were out shopping for Christmas lights when she spotted this Nativity scene and decided she had to have it.

Some years she would set it on the hi-fi set, and other years she'd put it on top of our upright piano. I can still picture how carefully she placed each figure.

When she died, I inherited the set, still in its original box. Over the years I have added some figures of my own: an angel with a horn, a donkey, a piper and various barnyard fowl. I now set the crèche on our dining room buffet.

The main figures are delicate papier-mache, and I try to be as careful with them as Mom was. My husband thinks I'm fussy, because I dust and wrap each figure before I put it away in the box. For me, it wouldn't be Christmas without the beloved Nativity scene.

one special night

By Jeanne Hawley, Grayslake, Illinois

Christmas was always special when I was a little girl, living at Sacred Heart Convent in Springfield, Illinois, in the 1930s. I'd go to bed early on Christmas Eve so I could get some sleep before attending midnight Mass.

But I usually was too excited to fall asleep. So instead, I'd look out my window into the clear, starry night and imagine seeing Santa in his sleigh.

I wore my prettiest clothes for attending Mass. The organ music and Christmas hymns filled the chapel—and my heart. I felt that Jesus must love me an awful lot to let me experience the moving beauty on this special night.

After Mass, I'd go down to open presents in the Candy Room, where I often helped Sister de Chantal sell candy to high school students after they ate their lunches. But first we'd eat olive, cheese and nut sandwiches cut in pretty shapes. They tasted so good that I didn't mind waiting to open presents!

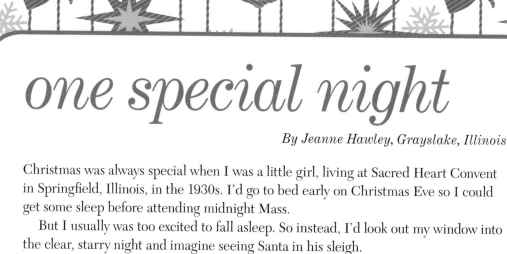

CONTENT IN CONVENT Author Jeanne Hawley warmly recalls Christmases at Sacred Heart Convent.

I always received lots of gifts, which Sister de Chantal would buy all year long for Christmas and birthdays. One year, I really wished for a bed for my baby doll. I opened all my gifts—new clothes, toys and books—but there was no place for my baby to lay its head. Then Sister led me to a dark corner in the room and lo and behold, there was a beautiful little blue baby bed, just big enough for my dolly. I'll never forget that feeling of joy that Santa had remembered my wish!

After opening all my gifts, we'd sit on a big rocking chair. Sister de Chantal would hold me close on her lap and rock me back and forth while a radio played Christmas carols and the Christmas tree lights cast a warm glow. My happiness at that moment knew no bounds. Soon I'd get sleepy and head back to bed, filled with the special happiness of Christmas.

a joyful noise

"One of the joys of my youth was caroling throughout the city of Charleston, West Virginia, before Christmas," writes the Rev. Kay Lowe McFarland of San Leandro, California. "Our choir from Boyd Memorial Christian Church rented a Greyhound bus, installed microphones and amplifiers on the roof, and took requests to sing for homebound friends and neighbors all over the city." In this 1947 photo, Kay, then 15, is at far left in front. Her mother, Mary Margaret Lowe, who was also the choir's director, is next to her, and her dad, the church's pastor, Rev. C. Oral Lowe, is standing in back.

CHAPTER FOUR

Festive Flavors

Sometimes it takes only the aroma of turkey roasting in the oven or spicy gingerbread men cooling on their baking sheets to bring the tastes of Christmas flooding back.

Janell Lowe's family holiday feasts brought lasting memories of good food and good company. "Christmas in the early 1950s at Grandma and Grandpa's was so exciting," she writes from Humboldt, Iowa. "Grandpa was an immigrant from Denmark and Grandma was from the Danish communities in Iowa, so we always had a traditional Danish meal. Grandma roasted the Christmas goose in her wood-burning kitchen stove. Her stuffing and pies were out of this world. Her special salad was peeled oranges with homemade whipped cream.

"There were so many of us that we'd eat in shifts. The men and boys would gather around the big dining room table first, and when they were done the women and girls would reset the table and refill the serving bowls for our turn. The visiting and eating went on for hours!

"After dinner, we'd exchange gifts. Then Grandma would give us each a piece of chocolate with a creamy filling. When our family left in the cold crisp night, it was with a sigh of contentment. We slept all the way home."

Turn the page for more sweet memories—and a baker's dozen of irresistible recipes.

a homemade Christmas

By Constance Guidotti
Cupertino, California

Pearl Lucas, known as Mimmy to her grandchildren, was my husband's grandmother, but she was a grandma to me, too. I met her in 1953, when I was just 16. In her print dress and crisp apron, with pure-white hair setting off her blue eyes behind gold-rimmed glasses, Mimmy looked like a fairy godmother.

Jim and I were high school sweethearts who married in 1955. The following year and every year until the early 1970s, it was tradition to enjoy homemade Christmas dinners at Mimmy's. It was her special gift of love to all of us.

Mimmy's husband, Henry, had died years before I met her. The couple had four children: my mother-in-law, Geneva, and her younger brothers, Homer, Harold and Howard. They and their own families, some two dozen children and adults in all, came to her house for this special holiday meal.

At that time, Mimmy lived in a clapboard cottage on the corner of McClelland Road and San Leandro Street in Cupertino. Her little house and lovingly tended garden sat in the middle of apricot and prune orchards.

Mimmy was a farm girl at heart. She not only prepared all the food from scratch, she grew most of it, too. Her Kenmore freezer was her most treasured modern convenience and the center for her yearlong preparations.

In early spring, yellow mustard carpeted her fields under clouds of blossoming fruit trees. By July 4, apricots were ready to pick— after the cherries but before the prunes. By midsummer, preparations for Christmas were in full swing.

First thing in the morning, Mimmy read the Bible while rocking in the oak chair in her living room. Then she went out while it was still cool to tend her garden and pick the day's crop of fruits and vegetables, which she cleaned and froze.

Summer afternoons, Mimmy settled into the rocking chair in the cool, dark living room to crochet the lace edging she used to trim the pillowcases she made for each woman in the family. (The men received store-bought

GARDENING GRANDMA Pearl Lucas, known as Mimmy to her grandchildren, spent many happy hours in her garden (top) and preparing for the family feast on Christmas Day (at left) in 1957 or 1958. In center photo, author Constance (right foreground) savored Christmas dinner at Mimmy's table in 1959. The author's son Harry is on the lap of her mother-in-law, Geneva, at the head of the table. Mimmy (half-hidden) is on the left.

Mimmy was a farm girl at heart. She not only prepared all the food from scratch, she grew most of it, too. Her Kenmore freezer was her most treasured convenience and the center for her yearlong preparations.

socks, and the kids were given crocheted slippers.)

As summer wore on, cucumbers were made into sweet pickles. When the figs from her tree were ripe, she candied them in a thick syrup. Each family would receive a Christmas goodie box that contained those candied figs, stuffed dried apricots, stuffed prunes and a festive homemade fruitcake.

As fall arrived, Mimmy canned September apples and froze October peaches. November pomegranates and persimmons completed the cycle. Then came the preparation of Christmas fruitcakes to be soaked in brandy.

After Thanksgiving, she made and froze the ravioli—one of the highlights of Christmas dinner, which she insisted on preparing without help.

Two days before Christmas, Mimmy made all the pies: pumpkin, apricot and apple pie from home-canned fruit. On Christmas Eve, she readied the cranberry relish and the turkey stuffing before the evening church service.

Early Christmas morning, she stuffed the turkey and put it in the oven, then spread crisp white cloths over the dinner tables. The windows were steamy from the cooking pots as we set out cut-glass dishes with goodies made the previous summer: watermelon pickles, sweet pickles, dill pickles and pickled crabapples.

Pasta sauce simmered while mashed potatoes and green beans from the summer's harvest stayed warm in the oven. The turkey in all its glory sat on the platter ready to be carved. The biscuits, green salad, cranberry sauce and gravy were made, and the ravioli was rising to the surface of the boiling water in a big pot on the stove.

Mimmy said grace before the meal began, about 1 or 2 p.m. She presided over everything, directing the serving of the food and the carving of the turkey.

And what a glorious feast it was! We all ate until we were stuffed.

These days, my husband follows in Mimmy's footsteps by growing all our fruits and summer vegetables. My sister-in-law Sandra carries on Mimmy's dinner tradition, preparing the homemade ravioli and hosting our holiday gathering as well.

Although Mimmy is no longer with us, her smile, her goodness and her generosity live on in all of us who were fortunate to share Christmas dinner at her table.

TASTY TRADITION Jim and Constance Guidotti and their children—from left, Tony, 4, Harry, 8, and Kim, 10—always had their picture taken in front of Mimmy's house on Christmas Day, this time in 1965.

"Here they come, Mom! And Jim won't need the wish-bone—they've got their PLYMOUTH!"

circa 1947

just like Mom's

Add these tried-and-true recipes to your menu and make Christmas even more memorable.

Just the mention of Christmas dinner can coax smiles and make mouths water. You think of the family gathering around the table, a sincere prayer of thanks before the meal, the same funny stories told year in and year out, and, yes, the wonderful food!

Maybe your favorite was juicy ham, turkey or beef, Mom's from-scratch rolls or a comforting side dish such as creamy mashed potatoes. Most likely, at least one of the dishes you loved as a child is on your Christmas menu today.

Shelby Keech can remember childhood Christmas feasts in detail. "When I was a kid in North Carolina during the '40s, Mother cooked all day long for Christmas Eve: fresh boiled ham, cooked collard greens, roast turkey with dressing and giblet gravy, chicken salad, sweet potatoes and potato salad," writes the Trenton, Florida, reader.

"Desserts included yellow layer cake with cooked chocolate icing, fresh coconut cake, pineapple cake, icebox fruitcake, plus chocolate, coconut and sweet potato pies."

If you'd like to add a new dish with old-fashioned flavor to your holiday table, consider one of these recipes for savory entrees and delicious sides.

Cranberry Raisin Relish

PREP/TOTAL TIME: 25 MIN.
YIELD: 2½ CUPS

- 2 cups plus 2 tablespoons sugar
- ½ cup water
- ½ cup orange juice
- 2 cups fresh or frozen cranberries
- ½ cup chopped dried apricots
- ½ cup golden raisins
- 1½ teaspoons grated orange peel

1. In a small saucepan, combine the sugar, water and orange juice; cook and stir over medium heat until sugar is dissolved.
2. Stir in the cranberries, apricots, raisins and orange peel; bring to a boil. Reduce heat; cover and simmer until the berries pop, about 15 minutes. Serve warm or chilled.

— Barbara Ford
Fort Gratiot, Michigan

Lemon-Dill Steamed Vegetables

PREP/TOTAL TIME: 20 MIN.
YIELD: 6 SERVINGS

- ¾ pound fresh baby carrots
- 4 medium new potatoes, quartered
- 6 fresh brussels sprouts, halved
- 2 tablespoons butter, melted
- 1 tablespoon lemon juice
- ½ teaspoon salt
- ½ teaspoon dill weed
- ⅛ teaspoon pepper

1. Place the vegetables in a steamer basket; place in a large saucepan over 1 in. of water. Bring to a boil; cover and steam for 10-12 minutes or until crisp-tender.
2. In a large serving bowl, combine the butter, lemon juice, salt, dill and pepper. Add the vegetables and toss to coat. Serve immediately.

— Page Alexander
Baldwin City, Kansas

Italian Christmas Turkey

PREP: 40 MIN.   BAKE: 3¾ HOURS + STANDING   YIELD: 16 SERVINGS (12 CUPS STUFFING)

- ½ cup butter, cubed
- 1 pound bulk Italian sausage
- 2 celery ribs, chopped
- 1 medium onion, chopped
- 1 package (14 ounces) seasoned stuffing cubes
- ¼ cup egg substitute
- 2 to 3 cups hot water
- 1 turkey (16 pounds)
  Salt and pepper to taste

1. In a large skillet over medium heat, melt butter. Add the sausage, celery and onion; cook and stir until meat is no longer pink. Transfer to a large bowl; stir in the stuffing cubes, egg substitute and enough water to reach desired moistness.
2. Just before baking, loosely stuff turkey with stuffing. Place remaining stuffing in a greased 2-qt. baking dish; cover and refrigerate. Remove from the refrigerator 30 minutes before baking.
3. Skewer turkey openings; tie drumsticks together. Place breast side up in a roasting pan. Rub with salt and pepper.
4. Bake, uncovered, at 325° for 3¾ to 4¼ hours or until a meat thermometer reads 180° for turkey and 165° for stuffing, basting occasionally with pan drippings. (Cover loosely with foil if turkey browns too quickly.)
5. Bake additional stuffing, covered, for 25-30 minutes. Uncover; bake 10 minutes longer or until a thermometer reads 160°. Cover turkey and let stand for 20 minutes before removing stuffing and carving turkey. If desired, thicken pan drippings for gravy.

— Elsie Laurenzo Palmer, Saratoga Springs, New York

*Gifts of time and love
are surely the basic
ingredients of a truly
merry Christmas.*

— PEG BRACKEN

Beef Tips & Caramelized Onion Casserole

PREP: 40 MIN. BAKE: 1½ HOURS
YIELD: 8 SERVINGS

- 4 pounds beef sirloin tip roast, cut into 1-inch cubes
- ½ teaspoon salt
- ½ teaspoon pepper
- 2 tablespoons olive oil
- 4 large sweet onions, halved and thinly sliced
- 3 tablespoons butter
- 4 garlic cloves, minced
- ⅔ cup all-purpose flour
- 2 cans (10½ ounces each) condensed beef consomme, undiluted
- 1 can (14½ ounces) reduced-sodium beef broth
- 2 tablespoons Worcestershire sauce
- 2 bay leaves
- ½ cup heavy whipping cream
- 8 slices French bread (½ inch thick), toasted
- 1 cup (4 ounces) shredded part-skim mozzarella cheese

1. Sprinkle beef with salt and pepper. In a large skillet, brown meat in oil in batches; drain. Transfer to a greased 13-in. x 9-in. baking dish.

2. In the same skillet, cook onions in butter over medium-low heat for 25-30 minutes or until golden brown, stirring occasionally. Add garlic; cook 2 minutes longer.

3. Stir in flour until blended; gradually add consomme and broth. Stir in Worcestershire sauce and bay leaves. Bring to a boil; cook and stir for 1 minute or until thickened. Pour over beef.

4. Cover and bake at 325° for 1 hour. Carefully stir in cream; discard bay leaves. Bake, uncovered, 25-35 minutes longer or until meat is tender. Place toast over beef mixture; sprinkle with cheese. Bake for 5 minutes or until cheese is melted.

— *Linda Stemen
Monroeville, Indiana*

Berry-Port Game Hens

PREP: 20 MIN. BAKE: 50 MIN. YIELD: 2 SERVINGS

- 1 large orange
- 2 Cornish game hens (20 to 24 ounces each)
- ½ teaspoon salt
- ½ teaspoon pepper
- 1 cup ruby port wine or grape juice
- ¼ cup seedless strawberry jam
- 5 teaspoons stone-ground mustard

1. Finely grate peel from orange to measure 1 teaspoon. Cut orange in half widthwise; cut a thin slice from each half. Quarter slices and set aside. Juice the orange to measure ¼ cup.

2. Loosen skin around hen breasts and thighs; place orange slices under the skin.

3. Place hens in a greased 13-in. x 9-in. baking dish. Sprinkle with salt and pepper. Bake, uncovered, at 350° for 40 minutes. Meanwhile, in a small saucepan, combine the wine, jam and orange juice. Bring to a boil. Reduce heat; simmer, uncovered, for 6-8 minutes or until slightly thickened. Stir in mustard and orange peel.

4. Set aside ½ cup sauce for serving; brush remaining sauce over hens. Bake hens 10-20 minutes longer or until a meat thermometer reads 180°, basting occasionally with pan juices. Warm reserved sauce; serve with hens.

— *Josephine Piro
Easton, Pennsylvania*

visions of sugar plums

Chocolate-covered cherries, French creams, peppermint candy canes, ribbon candy, orange slices and spice drops: At the mere mention of these words I can almost taste each candy. On Christmas morning, I couldn't wait to see what my stocking held. My favorites were the Country Inn confections filled with jam, nuts and chocolate in beautiful sugar shells. This candy was art! Each piece had its own distinct shape and flavor. It took me quite a while to memorize which shape held which flavor, and sometimes a surprise filling. This 1968 Sears Christmas Wish Book catalog page shows many of the distinctive hard candies you could buy for the holidays.

— *Cliff Miles, Orem, Utah*

Nibble-on Favorites to sweeten your snacktime

1 **Candy Cottage Kit.** Straight from the storybook land of Hansel and Gretel. Kit includes 2 lbs. of sugar candies, cardboard form and 12½x8-inch base. Complete instructions for assembly.
87 N 3524—Shipping weight 3 lbs.... Kit $1.99

2 **Christmas Candy Boxes.** Fill a few with our hard candy to keep on hand as holiday surprises for little visitors. Cardboard. 4x1x3 in. high.
87 N 3540—36 Boxes. Wt. 1 lb. 8 oz....Pkg. 79c
87 N 3541—100 Boxes. Wt. 4 lbs. 8 oz.... Pkg. $1.79

3 **Coconut Bonbons.** Sun-ripened coconut coated with whipped cream fondant. Favorite flavors .. chocolate, vanilla, lemon, strawberry. 4 lbs.
87 N 1532—Shpg. wt. 4 lbs. 8 oz..... Box $1.99

4 **Old-fashioned Ribbon Mix.** Delicate swirls of sweet treats and assorted hard candies in family-sized packages to make every day a holiday.
87 N 1500—3 pounds. Wt. 3 lbs. 8 oz. Pkg. $1.27
87 N 1501—6 pounds. Wt. 7 lbs..... Pkg. 2.49
87 N 1502K—30 pounds. Wt. 33 lbs. Pkg. 9.99

5 **French Creams.** Smooth, crystallized soft-sugar candy molded into miniature forms. Vanilla, lemon, orange, lime, raspberry, pineapple, maple and chocolate flavors. 2½ pounds in box.
87 N 1533—Shipping weight 3 lbs.... Box $2.49

6 **Sears Candy Mix.** Assorted hard candies. Individually wrapped. Great stocking stuffers.
87 N 1504—2 pounds. Wt. 2 lbs. 8 oz. Pkg. $1.09
87 N 1505—8 pounds. Wt. 9 lbs..... Pkg. 3.69
87 N 1506C—24 pounds. Wt. 27 lbs.... Pkg. 9.79

7 **Candy Canes.** Popular peppermint treats can dress up a Christmas tree, spice up holiday gift wraps, reward Mom's little helpers. Wt. 1 lb. 12 oz.
87 N 3532—6½-inch Canes. Box of 24. Box 98c
87 N 3533—3½-inch Canes. Box of 40. Box 98c

8 **Candy-filled Apothecary Jars.** Chocolate-filled mint straws in one, sugar shells filled with peanut butter, vanilla, fruit and chocolate in the other. 2 lbs. of candy in glass jars 10 in. high.
87 N 1513—Shipping weight 6 lbs....Set $2.29

9 **Old Fashion Penny Candy.** "Candy store" treats .. licorice babies, rock candy, liberty streamers, lemon drops, burnt peanuts. 4 lbs.
87 N 1569—Shpg. wt. 4 lbs. 8 oz.....Box $2.99

10 **Milk Chocolate Bells and Balls.** Solid chocolate. Foil wrapped. One lb. of each. From Belgium.
87 N 2548—Shpg. wt. 2 lbs. 8 oz.....Box $1.99

11 **Licorice Allsorts.** Chewy, nibble-sized treats from Bassett of England. Two pounds.
87 N 1573—Shpg. wt. 2 lbs. 8 oz.....Box $1.49

12 **Pail or Wastebasket filled with Mixed Candy.** Plastic containers 10½ in. high, each hold 5 lbs. of candy .. 2-lb. bag hard candy, 2-lb. bag cream and jelly candy, chocolate drops. Wt. 9 lbs.
87 N 1538—Pail.................Each $3.87
87 N 1541—Wastebasket.........Each 3.87

13 **Country Inn Filled Confections.** Jam, nut and chocolate in crisp sugar shells. 3-lb. tin. Shipping weight 4 pounds 8 ounces.
87 N 1503.............Tin $1.75 Sears 331

my favorite Christmas candy was

baking bliss

Oven-fresh delights serve up homemade flavor and old-fashioned goodness

When it comes to Christmas baking, colorful cookies often take center stage. But most holiday celebrations wouldn't be the same without the sweet raised rolls, tender cakes and festive pies Mom and Grandma made from scratch.

"Coming home from school to the aroma of bread fresh out of the oven was always a treat," recalls Patricia Hoard of Burton, Michigan. "But during Christmas baking time, it was even more special. Mother baked an individual loaf filled with raisins, cinnamon and nuts for each of us children. At the same time, she set aside extra dough and shaped it into small balls, which were deep-fried to a golden brown, then rolled in sugar. What a treat!"

Bring back the familiar flavor of holidays from your childhood with these foolproof recipes for sweet breakfast rolls, a cranberry-pear pie and irresistible individual fruitcakes.

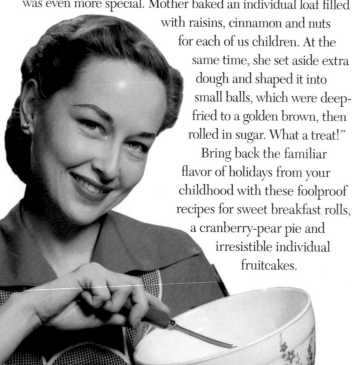

Partridge in a Pear Tree Pie

PREP: 30 MIN. + COOLING
BAKE: 40 MIN.
YIELD: 6-8 SERVINGS

- 1 can (15 ounces) pear halves, drained
- 1 package (12 ounces) fresh or frozen cranberries
- 1 can (8 ounces) crushed pineapple
- 1 1/2 cups sugar
- 3 tablespoons all-purpose flour
- 1/4 teaspoon salt
- 1/4 teaspoon ground cinnamon
  Pastry for double-crust pie (9 inches)
  Additional sugar, optional

1. Set aside five pear halves; chop any remaining pears. In a large saucepan, combine the chopped pears, cranberries, pineapple and sugar. Bring to a boil; cook and stir for 4-5 minutes or until some cranberries have popped. Cool for 30 minutes, stirring several times. In a bowl, combine the flour, salt and cinnamon. Stir in cooled cranberry mixture.

2. Line a 9-in. pie plate with bottom pastry; trim and flute edges. Spoon cranberry

ClassicStock.com

mixture into pastry shell; arrange pear halves on top. Bake at 400° for 35-40 minutes or until bubbly and crust is golden brown (cover edges with foil for last 15 minutes of baking if necessary). Cool on wire rack.

3. Roll remaining pastry. Using cookie cutters, cut out small leaves, small pears and a partridge. Place on an ungreased baking sheet; sprinkle with sugar if desired. Bake at 400° for 6-8 minutes or until golden brown. Place partridge in center of pie with leaves and pears around it.

— Jill Rens
Champlin, Minnesota

Cranberry-White Chocolate Cinnamon Rolls

PREP: 45 MIN. + RISING
BAKE: 30 MIN. + COOLING
YIELD: 16 SERVINGS

- 2 packages (1/4 ounce each) active dry yeast
- 2 cups warm water (110° to 115°)
- 1 cup butter, melted
- 1/2 cup sugar
- 2 teaspoons salt
- 5 to 6 cups all-purpose flour

FILLING:
- 1 cup butter, softened
- 1/2 cup packed brown sugar
- 2 teaspoons ground cinnamon
- 1 package (10 to 12 ounces) white baking chips
- 1 cup dried cranberries
- 1/2 cup chopped pecans

GLAZE:
- 2 cups confectioners' sugar
- 5 to 6 tablespoons heavy whipping cream
- 2 teaspoons vanilla extract

1. In a large bowl, dissolve yeast in warm water. Add the butter, sugar, salt and 4 cups flour; beat until smooth. Stir in enough remaining flour to form a soft dough.

2. Turn onto a floured surface; knead until smooth and elastic, about 6-8 minutes. Place in a greased bowl, turning once to grease the top. Cover and refrigerate overnight.

3. Punch dough down. On a lightly floured surface, roll into a 24-in. x 12-in. rectangle. For filling, combine the butter, brown sugar and cinnamon; spread over dough to within 1/2 in. of edges. Sprinkle with chips, cranberries and pecans. Roll up jelly-roll style, starting with a long side; pinch seam to seal.

4. Cut into 16 slices. Place cut side down in two greased 13-in. x 9-in. baking pans. Cover and let rise in a warm place until doubled, about 45 minutes.

5. Bake at 350° for 30-35 minutes or until golden brown. Combine glaze ingredients; drizzle over warm rolls. Cool on wire racks.

— Meg Marriott
Tacoma, Washington

Miniature Fruitcakes

PREP: 10 MIN.
BAKE: 1 HOUR + COOLING
YIELD: 1 DOZEN

- 3/4 cup sugar
- 1/4 cup all-purpose flour
- 1/2 teaspoon baking powder
- 1/8 teaspoon salt
- 1 1/2 cups chopped walnuts
- 1 cup chopped dates
- 3/4 cup chopped mixed candied fruit (about 4 ounces)
- 2 eggs, separated
- 1/2 teaspoon vanilla extract
  Halved candied cherries

1. In a large bowl, combine the first seven ingredients. Combine egg yolks and vanilla; stir into dry ingredients. In a small bowl, beat egg whites until stiff peaks form; fold into batter. Fill greased and floured muffin cups two-thirds full. Cover muffin tin tightly with heavy-duty aluminum foil.

2. Bake at 275° for 1 hour. Uncover; top with cherries. Bake 5 minutes longer or until a toothpick inserted near the center comes out clean. Cool for 5 minutes. Run a knife around the edges of each cup; remove to a wire rack to cool completely.

— Ruth Burrus
Zionsville, Indiana

a comfort food Christmas

Family recipes are cornerstone of holiday dinner through the decades.

Who doesn't remember eagerly pulling up a chair to a linen-draped table sagging beneath a feast of delicious Christmas dishes? Whether it was Mom's, Grandma's or Great-Aunt Ruth's table, heaping helpings of favorite foods waited to be savored.

Though menus shifted as new products came on the market and home cooks became more adventurous, holiday fare has always included beloved recipes passed down through the generations. With a taste for familiar flavors, 1960s families often relished the same dishes their forebears ate in the 1930s.

The platters and bowls also suggested our melting-pot beginnings, often combining American china or crockery with those reflecting the family's ethnic origins.

The main course almost always centered on an impressive cut of meat. Standing rib roasts reflected an English background, while those with German and Eastern European roots often chose roast goose. Turkey, a European favorite, appeared less often on Americans' Christmas menus because it had starred the month before on Thanksgiving. Dressed ducks, crown roasts of pork, legs of lamb and handsome hams—Hormel sold the first canned ones in 1926—also starred on dining room tables.

Rich gravy crowned comforting mashed potatoes. Relish trays and vegetables, such as mashed rutabaga and creamed onions or peas, rounded out the spread. If stuffing was served, its ingredients varied by region: Southerners used corn bread as their dressing base; oysters cropped up in coastal settings; and Midwesterners blended toasted white bread with celery, onion and sage.

The Great Depression and World War II, and the accompanying economic turmoil and rationing, had folks downsizing menus while still keeping the holiday spirit alive. Practical cooks used the ingredients they had on hand to serve the fanciest foods and desserts they could afford, such as wacky cake (an eggless, milkless confection) and mock apple pie (the Ritz Cracker version promoted by Nabisco in the mid-1930s).

circa 1945

DINNER AT GRANDMA'S Donald MacCallum, his wife, Connie, and sons Scott (center) and Peter took a moment before Christmas dinner in 1962 to have their picture taken by Donald's sister Margaret MacCallum of Moncton, New Brunswick. Grandma Mary is shown standing in back.

Thanks to convenience foods also introduced in the '30s—Birds Eye frozen vegetables, Campbell's cream of mushroom soup, fruity Jell-O—cooks found it easier to be creative. Molded gelatin salads and tomato aspics in Christmas reds and greens jiggled atop many a serving dish. The green bean casserole, invented in 1955 by Campbell Soup Co., remains a popular addition to holiday menus, as do candied yams, which boomed in the 1930s, when marshmallows became affordable for the masses.

In the postwar 1950s and 1960s, cream cheese, bacon and spinach were the foundation of an assortment of appetizers and side dishes. Homemakers spread cream cheese on celery, wrapped it in salami or dried beef and used it as a base for nut-crusted cheese balls. Bacon wrapped everything from chicken livers to dates and garnished spinach salads—a hip addition to 1960s tables that also featured a changing medley of crispy chow-mein noodles, mandarin oranges, sliced eggs and water chestnuts.

Grand-finale desserts—the ones likely to appear only at Christmas—differed by family, but plum puddings provided a Dickensian flourish in the 1930s. Bûche de Noël, a frosted log-shaped cake roll with cream or jelly filling, showed off the baker's artfulness. Pie choices ranged from pumpkin, apple and pecan to creamy creations, including banana cream, coconut custard, nesselrode (custard flavored with candied fruit, rum and whipped cream) and chess (a Southern specialty made with eggs, sugar and butter). Dense fruitcakes and hard-sauced gingerbread vied with multilayered whipped-cream tortes.

Although the menus may have changed with the times, Christmas dinners remain heartwarming gatherings that remind us of our origins, strengthen family ties and cook up delicious childhood memories.

our Christmas menu always included

_____

_____

_____

_____

_____

Christmas cookie classics

Helping Mom decorate cutouts earned boy some sweet rewards and merry memories.

By Dave Neimeyer, Fogelsville, Pennsylvania

In our house in the 1950s and '60s, the first sign of Christmas was when my mother started baking cookies. Oatmeal, chocolate chip, kiffles, spicy cow tongues, butterscotch cornflake cookies and other varieties came out of my mother's kitchen in succession.

However, it was the roll-out cookies that gave my older sister, Diane, and me the greatest opportunity to join in the preparation. Our mother would roll out the dough, and we'd select our favorite cookie cutters from among the reindeer, Santas, puppy dogs, Christmas trees, bells, stars, circles and gingerbread men. When there was no room for any more shapes, my mother would reroll the dough and we'd start to work on a new canvas. After rerolling once or twice, we baked any scraps of unused dough in whatever shape they happened to be—we called these "winger-wangers."

Once the shapes were cut, the decorating fun would begin! We'd put a little sugar in a small bowl and mix in a few drops of food coloring. As we grew imaginative, red and yellow became orange. Mixing other colors gave us brown, purple or black. This basic palette became the brown of reindeer hide, the red of Santa's coat or the yellow of a star. As quickly as we decorated each sheet of cookies, they were whisked into the oven to bake while we did our Picasso impressions on the next sheet.

When the cookies were done baking, they'd be placed on dish towels to cool. Of course, we had to make sure they had turned out OK. The best-tasting cookies were always the ones we tried fresh and hot from the oven.

We also had to make room on the towels for the next batch of cookies, which meant slowly rearranging the cooler cookies and "disposing" of those that didn't seem to fit, or had broken, or that just looked too tasty. Finally, they went into tins for later consumption. But it's a wonder any of them made it that far.

Create delicious memories with your children or grandchildren with these kitchen-tested recipes for traditional cutouts and other crowd-pleasing Christmas cookies. They're fun to decorate and even more fun to eat!

Sour Cream Sugar Cookies

PREP: 20 MIN. + CHILLING
BAKE: 10 MIN./BATCH
YIELD: 2 DOZEN

1/3 cup butter, softened
2/3 cup sugar
1   egg
1/3 cup sour cream
1/8 teaspoon lemon extract
12/3 cups all-purpose flour
3/4 teaspoon baking powder
1/8 teaspoon baking soda
1/8 teaspoon ground nutmeg
     Colored sugar or sprinkles,
     optional

1. In a small bowl, cream butter and sugar until light and fluffy. Beat in the egg, sour cream and extract. Combine the flour, baking powder, baking soda and nutmeg; gradually add to creamed mixture and mix well.

2. Divide dough in half. Shape one half into a 5-in.-long roll. Wrap in plastic wrap; place in a resealable plastic freezer bag. May be frozen for up to 3 months. Cover and refrigerate remaining dough for 1 hour or until easy to handle.

3. On a lightly floured surface, roll dough to ¼-in. thickness. Cut with a floured 2½-in. cookie cutter. Place 1 in. apart on a baking sheet coated with cooking spray. Sprinkle with colored sugar or sprinkles if desired.

4. Bake at 375° for 8-10 minutes or until bottoms are lightly browned. Cool for 1 minute before removing to a wire rack to cool completely.

5. To use frozen cookie dough: Remove dough from the freezer 1 hour before baking. Unwrap and cut into 12 slices. Place 1 in. apart on a baking sheet coated with cooking spray. Sprinkle with colored sugar or sprinkles if desired.

6. Bake at 375° for 8-10 minutes or until bottoms are lightly browned. Remove to a wire rack to cool.

— Kathleen Caddy
Tempe, Arizona

Gingerbread People

PREP: 25 MIN. + CHILLING
BAKE: 10 MIN./BATCH + COOLING
YIELD: 2½ DOZEN

6   tablespoons butter, softened
3/4 cup packed dark brown sugar
1/2 cup molasses
1   egg
2   teaspoons vanilla extract
1   teaspoon grated lemon peel
3   cups all-purpose flour
3   teaspoons ground ginger
1½   teaspoons baking powder
1¼   teaspoons ground cinnamon
3/4 teaspoon baking soda
1/4 teaspoon salt
1/4 teaspoon ground cloves
     Icing and candies of your
     choice

1. In a large bowl, cream butter and brown sugar until light and fluffy. Beat in the molasses, egg, vanilla and lemon peel. Combine the flour, ginger, baking powder, cinnamon, baking soda, salt and cloves; gradually add to creamed mixture and mix well. Divide dough in half. Refrigerate for 30 minutes or until easy to handle.

2. On a lightly floured surface, roll out each portion to ¼-in. thickness. Cut with a floured 4-in. gingerbread boy cookie cutter. Place 2 in. apart on greased baking sheets. Reroll scraps.

3. Bake at 350° for 7-9 minutes or until edges are firm. Remove to wire racks to cool completely. Decorate as desired.

— Joan Truax
Pittsboro, Indiana

Holiday Spritz

PREP: 30 MIN.   BAKE: 10 MIN./BATCH
YIELD: 7 DOZEN

1   cup butter, softened
1   cup confectioners' sugar
1   egg
1½   teaspoons rum extract
2½   cups all-purpose flour
1/4 teaspoon salt
     Colored sugar

1. In a small bowl, cream butter and confectioners' sugar until light and fluffy. Beat in egg

and extract. Combine flour and salt; gradually add to creamed mixture and mix well.

2. Using a cookie press fitted with the disk of your choice, press cookies 1 in. apart onto ungreased baking sheets. Sprinkle with colored sugar.

3. Bake at 375° for 6-9 minutes or until lightly browned. Cool for 2 minutes before removing from pans to wire racks.

— Lisa Varner
Charleston, South Carolina

Nativity Molasses Cookies

PREP: 1¼ HOURS
BAKE: 10 MIN./BATCH + COOLING
YIELD: 5 DOZEN

½	cup shortening
½	cup sugar
1	egg yolk
½	cup water
½	cup molasses
3¼	cups all-purpose flour
1	teaspoon baking soda
½	teaspoon salt
½	teaspoon ground ginger
½	teaspoon ground cinnamon
½	teaspoon ground cloves

ICING:

¾	cup sugar
1	egg white
⅓	cup water
⅛	teaspoon cream of tartar

1. In a large bowl, cream shortening and sugar until light and fluffy. Beat in the egg yolk, water and molasses. Combine the flour, baking soda, salt, ginger, cinnamon and cloves; gradually add to creamed mixture and mix well. Cover and refrigerate for 2 hours or until easy to handle.

2. On a lightly floured surface, roll out dough to ⅛-in. thickness. Cut with floured 2½-in. Nativity-themed cookie cutters. Place 1 in. apart on ungreased baking sheets. Bake at 350° for 10-12 minutes or until edges are firm. Remove to wire racks to cool completely.

3. In a heavy saucepan over low heat, combine the icing ingredients. With a portable mixer, beat on low speed for 1 minute. Continue beating over low heat until frosting reaches 160°, about 8-10 minutes. Pour into a small bowl. Beat on high speed until icing forms stiff peaks, about 7 minutes. Spread over cookies; let dry completely.

— Nancy Amann
Fountain City, Wisconsin

Chocolate-Mint Truffle Cookies

PREP: 25 MIN.
BAKE: 10 MIN./BATCH + COOLING
YIELD: ABOUT 2½ DOZEN

¼	cup butter, cubed
1	cup (6 ounces) semisweet chocolate chips, divided
1	egg
⅓	cup sugar
⅓	cup packed brown sugar
½	teaspoon vanilla extract
⅛	teaspoon peppermint extract
1	cup all-purpose flour
⅓	cup baking cocoa
¼	teaspoon baking powder
⅛	teaspoon salt
1	package (4.6 ounces) mint Andes candies, chopped, divided
2	teaspoons shortening, divided
½	cup white baking chips
	Optional toppings: chopped nuts, sprinkles and crushed candy canes

1. In a microwave-safe bowl, melt butter and ½ cup chocolate chips; stir until smooth. Cool slightly. Stir in the egg, sugars and extracts. Combine the flour, cocoa, baking powder and salt; gradually add to chocolate mixture and mix well. Fold in ¾ cup Andes candies.

2. Roll rounded tablespoonfuls of dough into balls. Place 2-in. apart on ungreased baking sheets. Bake at 350° for 8-10 minutes or until tops appear slightly dry. Cool for 1 minute before removing to wire racks to cool completely.

3. In a microwave, melt 1 teaspoon shortening and remaining chocolate chips and Andes candies; stir until smooth. Melt vanilla chips and remaining shortening in a microwave at 70% power for 1 minute; stir. Microwave at additional 10- to 20-second intervals, stirring until smooth.

4. Dip half of the cookies in melted chocolate mixture; allow excess to drip off. Place on waxed paper. Dip remaining cookies in melted vanilla mixture; allow excess to drip off. Place on wax paper. Immediately sprinkle with toppings of your choice. Let stand until set.

— Taste of Home Test Kitchen

coveted cookie house

In 1935, when I was 6 and living in Brillion, Wisconsin, my father,
a photographer, rented his old studio to a German baker, Paul Stellbrink.
A few weeks before Christmas, Mr. Stellbrink displayed a cookie house in
his front window that caused every child's eyes to open wide—especially
mine. It was about the most incredible thing I had ever seen, and I often
asked my parents what would happen to it after Christmas. I guess Mom
and Dad did a lot of talking, because they persuaded Mr. Stellbrink (shown
with me in this photo taken by my dad and tinted by my mom) to give
the sweet creation to me shortly after Christmas. What joy it gave me!

— *Art Neumeyer, Canyon Lake, Texas*

CHAPTER FIVE

Christmas Classics

Holiday entertainment has always been a great way to relax and set a festive mood, from movie magic on the big screen to can't-miss Christmas specials on TV. But above all, it was music that helped spread cheer and created memories.

Barbara Wallace of Traverse, Michigan, recalls Christmas Eve of 1945; the war had ended in August and the boys were coming home at last. "Once again, colorful Christmas lights beckoned through the windows of homes in our little seaside town of Old Orchard Beach, Maine. What a welcome sight after four long years of blackouts!

"I was 16 and having my first party—a Christmas Eve open house. At least 35 kids showed up to play games, sing carols and dance to my 78-rpm records. At 11:30, several of us pulled on our rubber overshoes, bundled up and trekked through the snow to midnight church service. We sang Christmas carols as we went, keeping time to the crunch of the snow packing under our feet.

"The service itself was beautiful, and walking home in the dark with the stars above, I knew this was the most glorious Christmas Eve I'd ever known. I could almost hear the angels singing, 'Peace on Earth.'"

Turn the page to read about popular holiday TV specials, movies and songs through the decades.

YEAR AFTER YEAR, THESE COLORFUL, ANIMATED HOLIDAY SPECIALS DELIGHT VIEWERS OF ALL AGES.

timeless television favorites

When a rather obscure movie studio escaped financial collapse, television fans became the richer for it. UPA, which had created the character of Mr. Magoo, was nearly bankrupt when promoter Henry G. Saperstein purchased it in 1960. Saperstein immediately switched the studio from animated movie shorts to TV production. The studio produced 130 Mr. Magoo TV shorts, then turned out the hour-long *Mr. Magoo's Christmas Carol*, an adaptation of the Charles Dickens story. It aired on Dec. 18, 1962, receiving critical praise and big ratings. Its success led to other animated Christmas specials, and they still appear each year, cherished by new generations and original fans alike.

Mr. Magoo's Christmas Carol
Composers Bob Merrill and Jule Styne offered a tune called *People*, but it was not included in the show. Instead, they used it in their popular Broadway musical *Funny Girl*. The song became a huge hit for Barbra Streisand.

Rudolph the Red-Nosed Reindeer
Based on the Robert L. May character and the Johnny Marks song, the show features Rudolph on the Island of Misfit Toys. It first aired on

Dec. 6, 1964, on the *General Electric Fantasy Hour*. Fearing overexposure for his song, Marks originally did not want to do the show, but was persuaded by co-producer Arthur Rankin, his neighbor. Also, the original show did not include Sam the Snowman, who narrates the story, but Burl Ives was brought in for star power and was rewarded with a hit song, *A Holly, Jolly Christmas*.

A Charlie Brown Christmas

The *Peanuts* characters help Charlie Brown find the true meaning of Christmas. CBS executives did not like the Biblical message and the lack of canned laughter, but Charles M. Schulz fought for the show. It received huge ratings when it first aired on Dec. 9, 1965.

To create the voice of Snoopy, director Bill Melendez spoke the lines and the tape was then sped up. Also, a trombone mimicking actors' inflections was used for adult voices.

I loved watching How the Grinch Stole Christmas! *But I always felt sorry for the little dog having to pull that giant sleigh. My mom always called roast beef "roast beast," like they did in the Grinch.*

— *Molly Kankel, Fort Wayne, Indiana*

How the Grinch Stole Christmas!

An adaptation of the Dr. Seuss book about a hateful creature who tries to prevent Whoville from enjoying Christmas, it first aired on Dec. 18, 1966.

Author Theodor Geisel did not want his book on TV, but director Chuck Jones talked him into it. Geisel didn't want Boris Karloff as The Grinch, either—he thought that would make the show too scary for young children—but again relented.

The Little Drummer Boy

An orphan drummer boy who hates humanity is changed when he meets the Three Wise Men on the road to Bethlehem. It first aired on Dec. 19, 1968.

Voices included actor Jose Ferrer as Ben and Greer Garson as Our Story Teller.

Frosty the Snowman

Based on Gene Autry's 1950 song, the show tells the story of a living snowman and a little girl protecting his hat from a greedy magician. It first aired on Dec. 7, 1969. This marked the last major film appearance for Jimmy Durante, who served as the narrator.

Santa Claus Is Comin' To Town

Here we're told the story of Santa Claus, starting when a baby named Kris is left on the doorstep of the toy-making Kringle family. It first aired on Dec. 14, 1970. The cast included movie veterans Fred Astaire as the narrator, Mickey Rooney as Kris and Keenan Wynn as Winter.

a whole new world

By Terri Ely, Bridgeton, New Jersey

The year was 1949, when I was 8 years old and my sister was 5. We were firm believers in Santa and went to bed early that Christmas Eve.

When Dad thought we were asleep, he began to weave his magic. Our ordinary living room would become a wonderland of toys and a glittering tree with trains and a miniature Christmas village beneath it.

We went to sleep expecting this traditional spectacle, and in the morning, flew down the steps and were thrilled, as usual, with the marvelous scene before us. We rushed over to the tree and began opening our gifts and stockings. When we finished, Mother and Dad said there was one more gift.

We looked around and didn't see anything. Then Dad fumbled with something on the other side of the room and we heard voices. Then we spotted it. Our first television! We whooped and hollered and were as excited as any two children could ever be.

Until then, we'd never dreamt that we would have a set of our own. In our neighborhood, only one child had a TV in her house. Fortunately for all of us, her mother let us watch a few programs with her every day. We thought that was heaven!

It's hard to describe to our grandchildren, who now have amazing technology at their fingertips, what a thrill that 10-inch black-and-white television was to us. Until then, like many families, we had one radio as the sole source of home entertainment. We didn't know that we were about to tune in to a whole new world of technology.

But for that moment, we relished the thought of having this simple TV. Watching it was like going to the movies in our own home. We all sat in awe and watched the holiday shows, one after another. When we finally got to sleep that night, my sister and I dreamed of the wonderful days ahead when we could watch *Frontier Playhouse*, *Howdy Doody*, cartoons and all the other shows we had heard about. Wow! This TV was the best Christmas gift ever.

BLACK-AND-WHITE BLISS Receiving a 10-inch television for Christmas was a dream come true for Terri Ely, shown here with her younger sister, Aunt Edna (left) and mother.

Jackie Gleason Originals by Manhattan® make dan-dan-dandy gifts

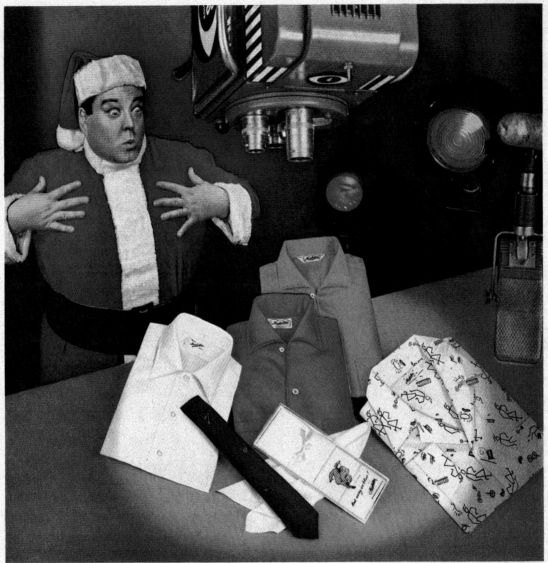

Jackie Gleason dress shirt, $5.00. Neckwear, $1.50. Sportshirt, $5.95. Handkerchiefs—set of 3, $1.50. "Dan-dan-dandy" Pajamas, $5.00, matching boxer shorts, $1.50.

And away we go . . . with the season's most thoughtful way to wish your "Mr. Saturday Night" a Merry Christmas. Give him smart new Jackie Gleason Originals. They're all by *Manhattan!* And they all display *Manhattan's* famous style, quality and craftsmanship, plus something more—Jackie Gleason's inimitable flair for luxury and comfort. For extra gift-giving fun, each shirt, sportshirt and handkerchief comes gift-packaged in a special Jackie Gleason gift package inscribed with Jackie's personal wishes for the Season's best. Mmmmmm, boy—these Jackie Gleason Originals are the greatest—and so are you for giving them! The Manhattan Shirt Company, 444 Madison Avenue, New York 17, N. Y.   ©1955 Cop. 1955 VIP Corp.

reel holiday spirit

FUNNY, SENTIMENTAL OR ALL-OUT
ENTERTAINING, MOVIES BRING HOME
THE WARMTH OF THE SEASON.

F or many families, watching a Christmas movie—or two or three—in the weeks leading up to the main event is as traditional as the Christmas tree. Here are a handful of holiday favorites that evoke the spirit of the season.

Babes in Toyland, 1934

The legendary comic duo of Stan Laurel and Oliver Hardy brought their brand of slapstick humor to this movie, which is based on a stage musical of the same name. The climax, in which wooden soldiers defeat the evil Silas Barnaby and his nefarious bogeymen and save Toyland, would warm even Scrooge's heart.

Holiday Inn, 1942

Honey-voiced Bing Crosby and dancer extraordinaire Fred Astaire star in this classic flick, in which two entertainers woo the lovely Marjorie Reynolds at the Holiday Inn, which is open—appropriately enough—only during holidays. Irving Berlin's *White Christmas* won the Academy Award for best original song.

The Bells of St. Mary's, 1945

Maybe it was the pairing of superstars Bing Crosby and Ingrid Bergman. Or the engaging rivalry between Crosby's affable Father O'Malley and Bergman's spunky but stubborn Sister Mary Benedict as they struggle to save St. Mary's, a failing Catholic school in New York City. Or possibly it's the tug-at-your-heartstrings ending. Whatever the case, this holiday flick remains as popular as eggnog.

It's a Wonderful Life, 1946

The gold standard of Christmas cinema, this iconic movie nicely gift wraps all the sentiments of the holidays in one beautiful, well-crafted package under the masterful direction of the legendary Frank Capra. Believe it or not, the film—which starred

Jimmy Stewart as the tortured yet redemption-bound George Bailey and Donna Reed as his saintly wife, Mary—was a box-office flop. It's now a classic, with amazing supporting roles for Lionel Barrymore as heartless Henry Potter, Thomas Mitchell as befuddled Uncle Billy and Henry Travers as Clarence Oddbody, the angel who gets his wings by helping George realize the true value of his life.

The Bishop's Wife, 1947

At first blush, this romantic comedy doesn't seem like a Christmas movie. It centers on Bishop Henry Brougham (David Niven), who's grown distant from his wife, Julia (Loretta Young), while consumed with building a new cathedral. An angel named Dudley (Cary Grant), who is sent in answer to the bishop's prayer for help, soon finds himself attracted to Julia, resulting in an unlikely love triangle. But the Christmas Eve ending, with Henry realizing what's really important in his life, makes this fantasy a holiday classic.

Miracle on 34th Street, 1947

Is there really a Santa Claus? This timeless favorite puts that question to the test as it spins a modern-day fable that's downright, well, miraculous. Edmund Gwenn won an Academy Award for best supporting actor as the besieged Kris Kringle, who is committed to an insane asylum for insisting he's the real Santa. The movie also features John Payne as attorney Fred Gailey, who defends Kris in court; Maureen O'Hara as Doris Walker, a Macy's events director and Santa nonbeliever; and a young Natalie Wood as her daughter, Susan, who, along with her mother, learns the importance of faith in a cynical world.

It's a Wonderful Life

the best Christmas movie ever

fairy-tale film

The holiday season of 1937 was made magic by a visit to Radio City Music Hall in New York with my mother to see Walt Disney's pioneering full-length animated feature *Snow White and the Seven Dwarfs*.

The lines of people waiting to get into the afternoon show extended outside the theater all the way to Fifth Avenue.

Once we got inside, the theater was already filled with thousands of people with coats and hats on their lap, waiting with great anticipation.

We were not disappointed. The movie's thrilling colors splashed onto the vast Radio City screen, and the golden musical score completed the fantasy. When the picture ended, the audience stood up and just cheered and cheered.

— *J.E. Gregory Murphy, Ridgewood, New Jersey*

Snow White: Sotheby's/AFP/Getty Images; Theater: Miemo Penttinen - miemo.net/Flicker/Getty Images

Snow White: Sotheby's/AFP/Getty Images; Theater: Miemo Penttinen - miemo.net/Flicker/Getty Images

96

Reminisce Christmas

"What a miracle you hide in a Christmas watch!"

said **ELIZABETH TAYLOR**

when she learned of

the DuraPower Mainspring

in **ELGINS** *that are*

so beautiful they won the

Fashion Academy Award!

Selected by the Fashion Academy of New York as "All-American Best-Dressed Woman" . . .
ELIZABETH TAYLOR
is co-starred in Metro-Goldwyn-Mayer's
"CONSPIRATOR"

THE
*DuraPower Mainspring**
ELIMINATES 99% OF ALL
REPAIRS DUE TO STEEL
MAINSPRING
FAILURES!

Lord Elgin and Lady Elgin
21 JEWELS   19 JEWELS

$6500

$5000

$6000

ELGIN *De Luxe*
17 JEWELS

$125.00 $125.00 $67.50 $67.50

Styled by Henslee

*Made of "Elgiloy" metal. Patent pending

Lord and Lady Elgins from $67.50 *to* $5,000.
Elgin De Luxe from $47.50 *to* $67.50. *Other*
Elgins from $29.75. *Prices include Federal Tax*

From your jeweler's whole array of precious gifts there's none quite so certain to be *style-correct* as an Elgin Watch. "Best-dressed women" like Miss Taylor . . . and "best-dressed men" like Lou Boudreau . . . wear Elgins proudly, for they are conscious of the fact that Elgin holds the Gold Medal Award of the Fashion Academy!

And Elgins are equally distinctive *inside*. Superb workmanship in every detail . . . and, to top it all, the miracle DuraPower Mainspring. *No other watch in the world has such dependable power for accurate timekeeping!* Don't forget that important fact when you choose a watch. Surely the one you love will be *happier* with an Elgin. See your jeweler's large selection of new Elgin styles.

ELGIN

TIMED TO THE STARS!

The genius of America to wear on your wrist

circa 1949

music casts a magical spell

LIKE TINSEL, HOLIDAY TUNES ADD SPARKLE.

Silent Night, *Joy to the World* and other classic carols are hard acts to follow, but 20th-century songwriters left us with a glorious garland of Christmas songs, too. Some are sacred, others romantic; some wise and wistful, others marvelously merry. Here are some of our favorites, from the '30s to the '60s, with just a sampling of the famous folks who recorded them and a bit about their history:

1934 *Santa Claus Is Coming to Town*, written by John Frederick Coots and Haven Gillespie, recorded by—among dozens of others—Ella Fitzgerald, Burl Ives, Dave Brubeck, Bruce Springsteen, the Boston Pops, Faith Hill and the California Raisins.

1940 or 1941 *White Christmas*, by Irving Berlin. Bing Crosby's achingly lovely '41 recording reigned for decades as the No. 1-selling single of all time, holiday-themed or otherwise. Despite rumors aplenty, pop historians say we'll probably never know exactly where or when Berlin penned it.

1941 *The Little Drummer Boy*, by Katherine K. Davis, recorded by Rosemary Clooney, the Trapp Family Singers and Whitney Houston. Also known as *Carol of the Drum*.

1943 *I'll Be Home for Christmas*, by Buck Ram, Kim Gannon and Walter Kent, recorded by Bing Crosby, Doris Day, Pat Boone, Elvis Presley, Johnny Cash, the Beach Boys, Toby Keith, Amy Grant and Placido Domingo. A favorite during World War II, it's still the holiday anthem of military personnel.

1944 *Have Yourself a Merry Little Christmas*, by Hugh Martin. The original lyrics were so sad that Martin was asked to rewrite them; the radiant result was immortalized by Judy Garland in the movie *Meet Me in St. Louis.*

1949 *Rudolph the Red-Nosed Reindeer*, by Johnny Marks, famously recorded by Gene Autry. The one and only Christmas song whose misheard lyrics spawned a modern TV holiday classic: the 1999 *Olive, the Other Reindeer.*

1950 *Silver Bells*, by Jay Livingston and Ray Evans, recorded by Jim Reeves, Jim Nabors, Alvin and the Chipmunks, Jack Jones, Regis Philbin, Stevie Wonder, Billy Idol and R.E.M.

1951 *It's Beginning to Look a Lot Like Christmas*, by Meredith Willson, recorded by Perry Como, the Fontane Sisters and Johnny Mathis. Years later, a version of the song was incorporated into Willson's Broadway musical *Here's Love*, which didn't do nearly as well as his beloved hit, *The Music Man.*

1953 *Santa Baby*, by Joan Javits, Philip Springer and Fred Ebb. Tongue-in-cheek charmer made famous by Eartha Kitt, later recorded by Les Paul, Madonna, Macy Gray,

Eartha Kitt

Calista Flockhart, Kylie Minogue, Taylor Swift and Miss Piggy.

1958 *Rockin' Around the Christmas Tree*, by Johnny Marks, recorded by Brenda Lee with an infectious joy that the Vienna Boys' Choir, Green Day and Miley Cyrus couldn't quite match.

1966 *We Need a Little Christmas*, by Jerry Herman. From the Broadway smash *Mame*, with the vivacious Angela Lansbury, later sung in the movie version by Lucille Ball.

my favorite Christmas song

traditions relived in stereo

In 1962, my dad went to a concert by a young man named Harry Belafonte at New York's Brooklyn College. Dad, who loved Belafonte's voice and his feel-good calypso arrangements, later bought the singer's album *To Wish You a Merry Christmas*, which would become a mainstay for decades.

Every Christmas Eve, Dad would raise the lid on the stereo, and Belafonte's lovely voice would fill the room. My brother, sister and I would know that it was time to bring in the Douglas fir and start decorating the tree and mantel.

I still have the Belafonte album, which I've framed and hung in my office. I play the album, now converted into a CD, throughout the year for periodic nostalgic lifts. The only thing missing is a scratch on one of the tracks, *I Heard the Bells on Christmas Day*. Believe it or not, I truly miss that scratch; it's a reminder of those special family holidays.

— *Philip Rossetto, New Tripoli, Pennsylvania*

jingle-bracelets ring

When I was a little girl back in the early 1930s, my mama played the piano and I sang along. She even sewed small bells onto circles of elastic to fit around the knuckles of each hand. At Christmas, when she played *Jingle Bells*, she wore these bracelets. I still have them and have worn them when I played this song.

— *Mildred Rapp, Frederick, Pennsylvania*

The Everett Collection

almost like being home

In World War II, I was a GI stationed at the New Orleans Staging Area and soon would be going overseas. My first Christmas away from home was coming, and I was homesick. A song that closely expressed my feelings had just come on the market, so I bought the record and mailed it to my mother. Mother didn't have a record player, so she took it to my Aunt Emma's. Mother told me later that they both cried. She said she felt like it is was me singing, but it was really Bing Crosby. That recording of *I'll Be Home for Christmas* is still one of the most popular holiday tunes. Whenever I hear it, I think of that lonely Christmas in New Orleans, and the world's greatest mother.

— *Joseph Weeks, Anaheim, California*

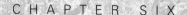

holiday moments

As you browse these festive photos,
hum along to the popular
Christmas tunes. They're sure
to put a song in your heart!

▶ This photo of me was taken at my parents' home
in 1963, the year my dad bought the latest—an
aluminum tree! He placed an electric color wheel
on the floor to spotlight the tree in different colors
as it rotated. — *Dorothy Seale, Shiner, Texas*

Silver and gold,
silver and gold
Mean so much more
when I see...
— Silver and Gold, 1964

*It's beginning to look
a lot like Christmas,
Toys in ev'ry store…*

— It's Beginning to Look
a Lot Like Christmas, *1951*

▲ Scenes like this one of warmly
dressed shoppers gazing at the
dolls, cars and other treasures in
the window of Woolworth's in the
1930s played out at five-and-dime
stores across the country every year
in the weeks leading up to Christmas.

◀ This picture of my sister, Judith (left),
and me was taken the Christmas of
1943 in our home in Antioch, Illinois.
We're holding a banner we made to
wish everyone a merry Christmas.

— *Uldine Andersen Wells
Inverness, Florida*

Brown Brothers

▲ Mary and I posed for this photo, which was used on the first Christmas card we sent as husband and wife in 1951. It was taken at the front door of our home in Fort Collins, Colorado, and printed by me. With this card, I began a tradition of making my own cards that lasted almost 30 years.

— *William Carnahan, Silver Spring, Maryland*

Chestnuts roasting on an open fire, Jack Frost nipping at your nose...

— The Christmas Song, 1944

▼ This is my daughter Karen on Christmas morning 1957 at our home in Wellesley, Massachusetts. She was having a great time playing with her new copper-clad pot, pan and teakettle on the play stove made from the box the cookware came in.

— *Roy Johnson*
Saxonville, Massachusetts

▲ I was so proud of this snowman that my parents and I built in the yard of the home we rented in West Haven, Connecticut, in 1940 when I was 9. We used sticks and stones to give the snowman some personality and found an old bucket to use as a hat.

— *Peggie Kamm Bergantino*
Northford, Connecticut

▲ These enthusiastic choirboys appear to be singing loud and proud during church services, a custom cherished by both children and adults in churches large and small on Christmas Eve and Christmas morning.

▶ This photo always makes me think Santa wanted to be sure he wasn't chilly, with his cap and beard covering everything but his eyes! I know our two daughters, Dianne and Lou Ann, were warm in their new mittens and happy with their Christmas stockings when this was taken in 1963 in Dyersville, Iowa.
— *Lois Hullermann, Fennimore, Wisconsin*

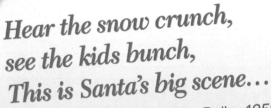

Hear the snow crunch,
see the kids bunch,
This is Santa's big scene...

— Silver Bells, *1950*

▶ I told my son Chuck that if he wanted a Christmas tree, it was his turn to go out in the woods and cut one down. He was ready and willing. The photo was snapped in December 1970, when we lived in the country near Middleburgh, New York.

— *Robert Siple Sr.*
Central Bridge, New York

◀ In 1962 and 1963, my brother, Rodney, his family and I converged on our parents' small two-bedroom home in Youngstown, Ohio, for the Christmas holidays. We had a good snowfall in 1962, so we built a snow family. Pictured are Tracey, Jody and Troy with their dad, Rodney. It was an excellent way to burn off the children's excess energy and give our parents a chance to relax while we were outside.

— *Ray Wylam*
Fairborn, Ohio

◀ It was Christmas 1961 when this photo of me and my sister, LaRee Johnston (right), was taken at Wolf & Dessauer in Fort Wayne, Indiana. It was an adventure to go there because they had many animated holiday figures in the windows. My favorites were the ice-skaters. Seeing Santa was a bonus.
— *Monica Davis, Wren, Ohio*

▼ Christmastime in the city, like this scene of Times Square in New York City in 1939, is a wonderful thing. The decorated storefronts, the shoppers bustling, the anticipation in the air: It's an exciting scenario that plays out across the country.

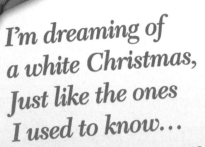

*I'm dreaming of
a white Christmas,
Just like the ones
I used to know...*

— White Christmas, 1940 or '41

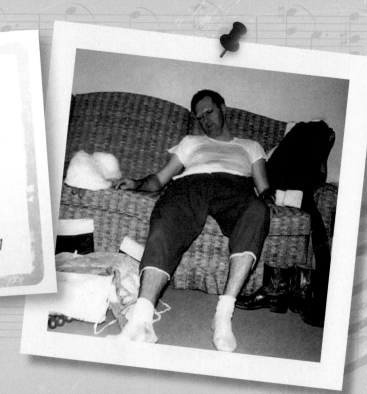

▲ While living in Scottsdale, Arizona, in the mid-1960s, I played Santa Claus for families, visiting a dozen homes on Christmas Eve. Each time, I jingled my sleigh bells, walked in and addressed the children by name, then presented them with gifts their parents had left outside the door. The reward for me was the surprise and delight on their faces when they'd hear Santa call their names. Being jolly was bit taxing after two hours and left me hoarse from all those hearty ho-ho-ho's. Returning home, I'd shed the costume and collapse on the couch. — *Jim Doyle Chambersburg, Pennsylvania*

◄ My brother, Robert (right), and I had our picture taken next to our Christmas tree in 1925 in Dayton, Ohio. I was 3 that year and he was 2. We're surrounded by toys, including a top, a drum, trains, alphabet blocks and two toy telephones. The photographer tinted this black-and-white photo. — *Jerome King Dayton, Ohio*

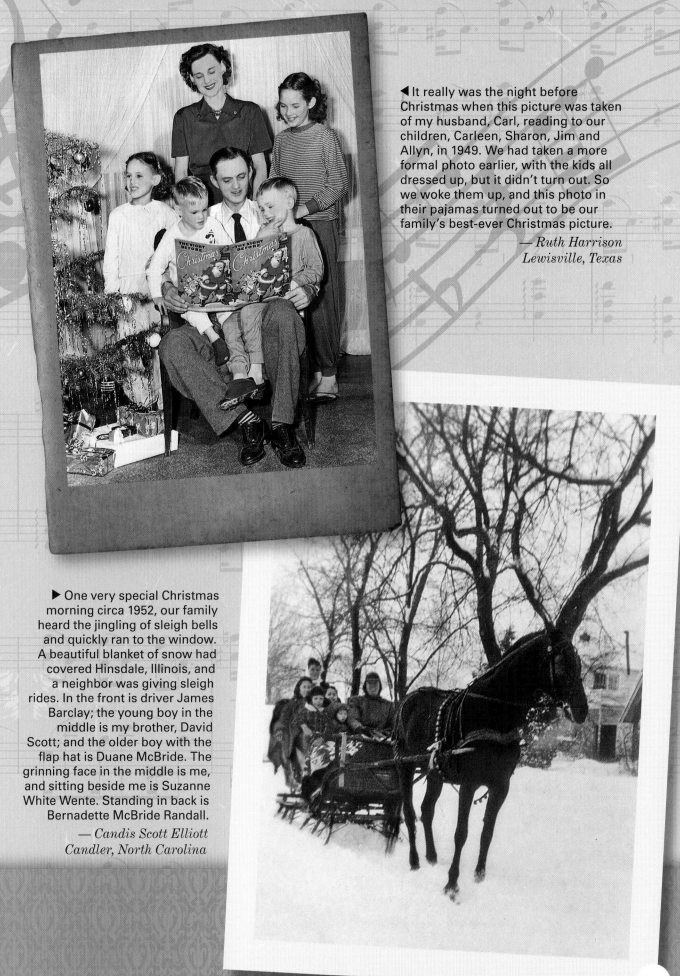

◄ It really was the night before Christmas when this picture was taken of my husband, Carl, reading to our children, Carleen, Sharon, Jim and Allyn, in 1949. We had taken a more formal photo earlier, with the kids all dressed up, but it didn't turn out. So we woke them up, and this photo in their pajamas turned out to be our family's best-ever Christmas picture.

— *Ruth Harrison*
Lewisville, Texas

► One very special Christmas morning circa 1952, our family heard the jingling of sleigh bells and quickly ran to the window. A beautiful blanket of snow had covered Hinsdale, Illinois, and a neighbor was giving sleigh rides. In the front is driver James Barclay; the young boy in the middle is my brother, David Scott; and the older boy with the flap hat is Duane McBride. The grinning face in the middle is me, and sitting beside me is Suzanne White Wente. Standing in back is Bernadette McBride Randall.

— *Candis Scott Elliott*
Candler, North Carolina

*All is merry and bright,
So hang your stockings
and say your prayers…*

— Here Comes Santa Claus, *1947*

▼ This picture was taken by my husband, Bob, on Christmas 1947. Our sons Gary, 3, and Doug, 1, had been told that Santa Claus comes down the chimney on Christmas Eve with a bag of toys, and they were looking for him. They were in their Dr. Denton pajamas with the bottoms that opened up.

— *Thelma Dickson*
Takoma Park, Maryland

◀ Prayers—whether at church services, in pageants or at youngsters' bedsides—took a more fervent tone at Christmastime. Here, three sisters pose with folded hands in front of the Christmas tree in 1956.

▼ My sister, Eileen, and I are pictured here with Santa in his sleigh in 1930. The photo was taken at one of the department stores in downtown Chicago. Back in those days, every department store had its own Santa Claus.

— *William Otten Jr.*
Lake in the Hills, Illinois

MERRY CHRISTMAS

Want a plane
that loops the loop,
Me, I want a hula hoop…

— The Chipmunk Song
(Christmas Don't Be Late), *1958*

◄ Our daughter, Joy, 5, was so excited on Christmas Eve 1964 that she just kept jumping up and down. Santa "just happened" to deliver presents to our home in West Allis, Wisconsin, while she and her brother, Joe, 3, were taking a bath. That's why her hair is wet!

— *Dolores Kastello*
Waukesha, Wisconsin

◄ Planes, trains and bikes: This store's window display seems to have most anything a young boy could wish for at Christmas. And from the look of the model airplanes, any of them could likely "loop the loop" and more.

► This photo was taken in 1965 at the home of my mother-in-law, Carol Greene, in Chilhowee, Missouri. The older boy is my husband, Dale Rush. From their expressions, both he and his younger brother, Jeff, look thrilled about their presents they're about to open.

— *Karla Rush, Carthage, Missouri*

> *He sees you when you're sleeping, He knows when you're awake…*
>
> — Santa Claus Is Coming to Town, *1934*

► This is me at age 22 months waiting for Santa on Christmas Eve in 1948. My parents, Arthur and Clara Kendrick, used the photo on their Christmas card that year. World War II had been over for just three years and most people in Boligee, Alabama, were not in the best of financial shape, so it's amazing they were able to have a personalized Christmas card made. The picture was taken in the big farmhouse where my grandparents lived.

— *Steven Kendrick, Louisville, Tennessee*

◄ I remember the fragrance of the balsam fir tree laden with glass ornaments, large multicolored lightbulbs and long strands of heavy foil tinsel. But I mostly remember the people, the laughter and the traditions. The gathering of family and friends is what truly made Christmas. I'm pictured here with our firstborn son, Michael, in 1956. He was just 1 month old when the slide was taken at our home in Fall River, Massachusetts.

— *Pauline Sirois Berube Tiverton, Rhode Island*

▶ This picture of our four children with Santa was taken at Sears in North Hollywood, California, in 1961. Gregory was 21 months old and none too happy. Kathleen (left) was 8½, Mark was 3½ and Sandra was 6½. Years later, in 1994, Sandy couldn't resist using this photo to put together a Christmas card for her brothers and sister with the caption, "Have you ever noticed that there's always someone who just can't get into the spirit?"

— *Janet Novy*
Cypress, California

◀ Decked out in her wings and robe for the school play, Lore Warren of Hayward, California, really was an angel on this Christmas in the 1930s. She says her father made the dollhouse, which had lights, and her mother made the doll clothes.

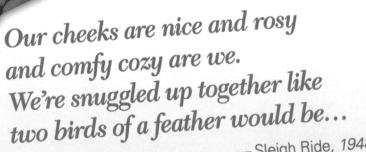

*Our cheeks are nice and rosy
and comfy cozy are we.
We're snuggled up together like
two birds of a feather would be...*

— Sleigh Ride, *1948*

▼ I'm definitely dressed for the cold in this picture with Santa taken Dec. 20, 1949. I was 19 at the time and employed at J.C. Penney in Minneapolis.

— *Margaret (Schwartz) Burke*
Anchorage, Alaska

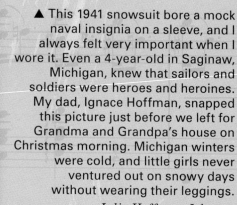

▲ This 1941 snowsuit bore a mock naval insignia on a sleeve, and I always felt very important when I wore it. Even a 4-year-old in Saginaw, Michigan, knew that sailors and soldiers were heroes and heroines. My dad, Ignace Hoffman, snapped this picture just before we left for Grandma and Grandpa's house on Christmas morning. Michigan winters were cold, and little girls never ventured out on snowy days without wearing their leggings.

— *Julie Hoffman Johnson*
Evansville, Indiana

▲ The gentleman in this picture had a tree farm about 20 miles south of Allentown, and we visited him every December for many years. After he helped me put the tree in our 1953 Pontiac, he posed with my daughters, Janice (left), and Sandra, who couldn't wait to get their prize home to Mom. That Christmas tree in 1957 was the best ever!
— *John Spangler*
Hanover, Pennsylvania

◄ In 1940, my dad insisted we needed a Christmas photo for our relatives in Switzerland. Frustrated with the lack of snow in West Haven, Connecticut, that year, he had my sisters, Shirley and Frances, and me dress in warm outfits that Mom had made and pose under hot photography lamps. I don't believe those cotton balls fooled anyone.
— *Peggie Kamm Bergantino*
Northford, Connecticut

Christmas Eve will find me Where the love-light gleams…

— I'll Be Home for Christmas, *1943*

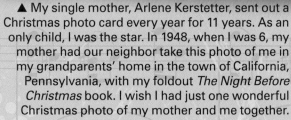

▲ My single mother, Arlene Kerstetter, sent out a Christmas photo card every year for 11 years. As an only child, I was the star. In 1948, when I was 6, my mother had our neighbor take this photo of me in my grandparents' home in the town of California, Pennsylvania, with my foldout *The Night Before Christmas* book. I wish I had just one wonderful Christmas photo of my mother and me together.

— *Virginia Ann Kerstetter Butler, Milton, Pennsylvania*

▼ In the days when members of most families lived within a few miles of each other, gatherings at holiday dinners were the norm, as was posing for a picture before the meal. This photograph—taken, I believe, in 1955—was at my cousin's home in Marion, Indiana. I'm standing at far left. Also standing are (from left) Frank Diodore, my cousin Kathryn's husband; my aunt Viola Dare; my sister, Judith Bruning; my parents, Ann and Thomas Miller; and Kathryn. Seated are my maternal grandmother, Bessie Dare, and Uncle Wallace Dare. Just looking at this photo brings back so many warm memories.

— *Larry Miller, Lakewood Ranch, Florida*

▲ Little Darla Lampton Barrow, now of Wadesville, Indiana, appeared to be getting ready for a long winter's nap in this photo from the early 1960s. She was enjoying a pre-Christmas overnight stay at her Aunt Midge and Uncle Ed Crawford's home in Newburgh.

— *Jim Crawford, Newburgh, Indiana*

CHAPTER SEVEN

Season of Giving

The old adage that it's better to give than receive may sound like a cliché, but it's true nonetheless. Just ask Barbara Bergen of Muskego, Wisconsin, who fondly recalls the Christmas her brother Paul cherishes the most—and not because he received his first two-wheeler bicycle.

"During the 1940s in Muskego, Paul (at right) saved part of his weekly allowance to buy Christmas gifts for everyone for the first time. As Christmas drew near, he enlisted his three older sisters to help him shop at the local Woolworth's.

"We helped him wrap the presents, which he put under a little decorated 'tree'—the top from our tree, which Dad cut off because it was too tall.

"On Christmas morning, Paul was so excited about handing out gifts that he never saw his new bike. He passed by it several times—even touched it once—but was so enthralled with giving presents that he didn't notice it until later.

"That Christmas always reminds me how important it is to give children a chance to feel the joy of giving."

The season's generosity manifests itself in many ways, as the following stories illustrate.

choosing Mother's gift

By Dorothy Sidney Smith
Madison, Indiana

Christmas looked to be a little out of kilter for our family in 1939. Certainly, we had enough to be thankful for, having just purchased a house in Chicago after years of saving money and searching. I even had my own room, which was a big thing for an 11-year-old girl. And there was also a basement room where my brother, Philip, 9, and I could play pingpong and hang out.

But a lot of things seemed to go wrong that Christmas. We moved on a chilly December day, and before we even finished unpacking all the boxes, Mother got sick. In fact, she went to bed, which told my brother and me that she was really sick.

My father, already worried about the expense of the move, was now even more concerned about my mother. On top of all that, I was dreading the first of the year, when I would start attending a new school. As a sixth-grader, I found that a terrifying thought. My brother and I hadn't met the neighborhood kids and missed our old friends back home. Even with Christmas right around the corner, I was down in the dumps.

But my father set things right for me. "I need your help," he said, talking to me as though I were an adult (which I secretly felt I already was). He explained his dilemma: Mother hadn't had time to shop for Christmas gifts before she fell ill, and he wanted me to pick out toys for Philip. I enthusiastically agreed.

Heady with this newfound responsibility, I set out with Father on a blustery Dec. 23 evening. We walked through the shopping district and talked about this and that. I don't much remember what toys we picked out for Philip, though they probably were army men and tanks, games and books. But I felt my father's mood lifting as the minutes passed.

Then, wonder of wonders, Father asked me to pick out my mother's gift! We entered a jewelry store, where I saw glass display cases filled with pins and necklaces glittering on dark velvet. Then I spotted the gift of gifts: a light-blue musical powder box. When

MEMENTO FOR MOM
Author Dorothy Sidney Smith
took pride in selecting just the
right Christmas gift for her
mother, Dorothy Alexander
Sidney, shown above on
Crandon Avenue in Chicago

we turned the key underneath it and lifted the decorated lid, it played a soft classical tune. I was ecstatic—what a magical gift for Mother!

By Christmas Day, Mother was feeling better and joined us around the Christmas tree. I don't remember what presents I received or who picked them out. But I do remember the joy my brother found in his gifts and the way my mother looked when she heard the soft music coming from the powder box.

That Christmas, I moved from childhood through the doorway to adulthood. And every Christmas from then on, my father always asked me to help him pick out a gift for Mother. It was his special gift to me.

YULETIDE SPIRIT Author Dorothy and brother Philip visit with Santa on his sleigh (below). This hand-painted Christmas card (right) is an example of those the author's mother made for family and special friends.

Then, wonder of wonders, Father asked me to pick out my mother's gift! We entered a jewelry store, where I saw glass display cases filled with pins and necklaces glittering on dark velvet. Then I spotted the gift of gifts: a light-blue musical powder box.

From our fireside to yours comes this wish for a very Merry Christmas 'd a Happy New Year. The Sidneys

the favorite present I gave

_____

_____

_____

_____

_____

PAINTED FOR PLYMOUTH BY NORMAN ROCKWELL

"Merry Christmas, Grandma...we came in our new PLYMOUTH!"

circa 1950

homespun and from the heart

Joyous smiles and warm memories result when gift-giving is in the caring hands of family members.

Handcrafted with love

In 1940, not too long after the Great Depression, our family was short on money as Christmas approached. My dad was a truck gardener and raised chickens, so we always had enough to eat. But we seldom received more than one present each, plus a stocking with a piece of fruit and some hard candy.

My brothers and sisters and I weren't expecting much that year, but as a hopeful 6-year-old (pictured above left), I still looked for presents in the Sears and "Monkey Wards" catalogs. I was especially drawn to a picture of the most beautiful little barn, complete with small farm animals and a fence. I wanted it so badly, but Mom and Dad told me it would take a miracle to get it.

On Christmas morning, we kids found one small present each. I didn't see anything for me until I looked behind the tree. There was a barn, all right—but not the one in the catalog. It was much better!

Howard, my oldest brother, who had just joined the Army, had spent many evenings after I went to bed working on the barn, the fence and the animals to go with it. Looking back, I realize how much he must have loved me to take so much time and energy to make that Christmas special for me.

—*John Sharp, Danville, Indiana*

Daughter's gift spoke volumes

My mother-in-law was a Polish immigrant who spoke English with a heavy accent. Much to her chagrin, only her two oldest children learned to speak Polish, while the other three—including my wife—did not. Her grandchildren didn't speak Polish, either, so at family gatherings we all spoke English, even though we followed Polish traditions.

At the time, I worked with a number of Polish men. For Christmas 1952, I asked one of my co-workers to teach me to say in Polish, "Merry Christmas and Happy New Year." In turn, I taught our 3-year-old daughter the phrase.

On Christmas Eve, as we were gathered in my mother-in-law's front room, with wrapping paper, games and toys strewn about, I asked for quiet and gave my daughter her cue. She stood in front of her grandma and recited the words perfectly. Everyone laughed and applauded.

But we all got lumps in our throats when we saw tears coursing down her grandma's cheeks as she started talking to my daughter in Polish.

To this day, "Merry Christmas and Happy New Year" are the only words my daughter can speak in Polish. But when she does so at the holidays, I know that, somewhere, her grandma cries tears of joy.

—*Clifford Zobel, Milwaukee, Wisconsin*

Meal came special delivery

Back in 1957, I was scheduled to work from 2 to 10 p.m. on Christmas Day at the C & P Telephone Co. in Baltimore. It would be the first time I'd miss Christmas dinner at home.

My mother told me to call her as soon as I knew what time I'd be taking a lunch break. When I called, she told me to go down to the lobby when lunch started. I did, and found my brother-in-law Artie with a plate of food, wrapped up and hot off the table.

I went back upstairs and unwrapped the plate, which held a little of everything Mom had fixed for dinner. All the other girls were sitting at the lunch table with their cold sandwiches!

I got teased about that for a long time, but I didn't care. My mother was always doing nice things for people she loved. She was a very special person and made sure I still felt like part of the family, even though I wasn't at the table for Christmas dinner.

—*Donna Ruby Osterkamp*
Middle River, Maryland

Handmade items keep giving

In 1931, when I was 6, our family lived in Buffalo, New York. It was during the Depression, and my father, who was a carpenter, made a doll crib, high chair and ironing board for me for Christmas. My mother made the bedding for the crib. This picture (below) shows me with all my wonderful presents in front of our Christmas tree.

When my brother, John, was born 12 years later, he slept in the crib for several months.

I kept all three pieces, and in 1954 I gave them to my oldest daughter for her dolls. Ten years later, they went to her sister. In 1971, the furniture was repainted and passed on to my granddaughter, and finally to my youngest son's daughters. The items my father built with his own hands nearly 80 years ago have brought my family a lifetime of enjoyment.

—*Eleanor Maurer Crashell, Phoenix, Arizona*

Dad fashioned fireman's helmet

When I was a boy, Christmas at our row house in Philadelphia was always the most exciting time of year. I eventually grew to learn the real significance of Christmas beyond just giving and receiving gifts—but as a boy, the toys I wanted were always the focus.

In 1941, Santa brought me a green pedal car, not the fire engine I wanted. My dad wasn't making much money at the time, so even the car was probably a stretch for us financially. But the next Christmas, I received that long-awaited shiny red fire chief's car with a bell on the hood.

To top it all off, the car came with a very realistic fireman's helmet that wasn't available in any store—because Dad had made it! Back in those days, Mom used a lot of Crisco, and an empty can—rigged up with a felt liner and a leather chin strap—provided the perfect material for this headgear. It was truly a work of art.

A couple of years went by before I realized that my "new" vehicle was really an old green toy car with an impressive bright-red paint job and some new white stripes and lettering!

I have a picture that shows me at age 4 (above) proudly wearing the fireman's helmet in front of the Christmas tree. My thoughtful father, Harry Deaver, clearly knew how to keep Christmas.

—*Ken Deaver, Dillsburg, Pennsylvania*

our Christmas of plenty

By Peter Avalos, Newark, California

As Christmas approached in 1942, my cousin and I were living with my grandparents in a dirt-floor garage by some railroad tracks in San Lorenzo, California. I was 10 years old, and we had moved there from Los Angeles.

My grandparents raised my cousin and me, both of us orphans. Times were very lean. A wood-burning stove in the middle of the room provided heat, we slept on two beds without mattresses, and our furniture consisted of wooden crates from a nearby cannery.

A few days before Christmas, welfare workers brought us some clothes and canned food. On Christmas Day, I put on some of the ill-fitting clothes and set out for Mass at St. John's Catholic Church.

After Mass, I stayed to pray. Suddenly, I felt a hand on my shoulder. A man said something to me in a foreign language and handed me a $10 bill. I couldn't contain my excitement as I ran home.

I gave the money to my grandparents, and we went to a little store and bought flour, rice, beans, lard and one chicken. Then Grandma cooked us an unforgettable meal on the woodstove: fresh tortillas, chicken *mole*, *frijoles de la hoya* (pot beans) and rice. For dessert, she made *capirotada*, a bread pudding, and we drank *atole*, a thick, gruel-like drink garnished with a cinnamon stick for flavor.

Afterward, since we had no television or radio, we sat around the stove and told stories. There were no presents or Christmas tree, but that night I slept as tranquilly as a child with an abundant life. It was a happy and innocent time in my life, thanks to my grandparents, Mexican immigrants who couldn't speak, read or write English, yet worked hard to provide for two orphaned boys.

You cannot teach love; you demonstrate it. And in their own simple way, that's what my grandparents did that night—and every day. I hope everyone has such a fond Christmas memory on which to reflect.

gleeful giving

Little Pamela Lichty got a big laugh from sister Susan over a present on Christmas morning 1954. Bob Lichty of Vacaville, California, shared the photo, which was taken at the family's home at Travis Air Force Base, also in California, where Bob was stationed at the time.

the gift that meant the most to me

caroling touched a chord

By Carol Devlin, Evergreen, Colorado

In 1949, when I was 6 years old, I received a most unexpected and precious gift while singing Christmas carols with my music teacher and classmates in Hill City, Kansas.

Bundled up warmly, we planned to sing one song at each house we visited. At the first house, the teacher rang the bell and asked the man who answered the door if we could sing a carol. He gathered his family at the door to hear us sing, and they applauded warmly when we finished. What fun!

We continued down the street. No one turned us down, and I felt as though we were doing something wonderful.

Then we came to a house where an elderly woman answered the door, wearing a housedress adorned with blue flowers. She had curly white hair and a wrinkled face, and smelled just like the rose bath powder we used whenever we took a bath at my grandma's house. I felt a twinge of love for this lady as she stood behind her screen door and agreed to hear us sing.

As we sang *O Holy Night*, tears began to stream down the woman's cheeks. She smiled and stood perfectly still. Unsure of how to react, some of us lost our place in the song, and others stopped singing altogether. Our teacher jumped in to sing with us, and we somehow managed a ragtag finish. I was absolutely dumbfounded.

"I'm sorry you're seeing me cry, children," the woman finally said. "Don't be upset. I'm very happy. Your song was lovely and one of my favorites. I'm alone now—my family is all gone. You don't know what it means to me to have you visit me and not feel forgotten. You've done something more wonderful than you'll ever know."

My teacher opened the screen door and gave the woman a hug. Then she held the lady's hand and helped her step down onto the porch, where she gave each of us a soft, warm, good-smelling hug. She thanked us for the song and wished us a merry Christmas.

As we headed down the sidewalk toward the next house, I looked back and saw the woman still standing in her doorway. She gave me a cheerful smile and waved. Our teacher looked as if she might cry. As we started to sing at the next house, a rousing round of *Deck the Halls*, her voice came out a little squeaky.

That woman thought we did something nice for her that day. But what she did for me lasted a lifetime.

TOUCHING TUNE A grateful listener made a big impact when 6-year-old Carol Devlin caroled with classmates.

Everybody knows the sign of good coffee

**WONDERFUL IN
INSTANT FORM
TOO!**

One warmhearted holiday gesture deserves another. And so, after the Christmas carols are sung, it's Maxwell House Coffee time. There's so much good cheer, such warm hospitality in every fragrant cup. No other coffee has that wonderful "Good to the Last Drop" flavor, because no other is made by the Maxwell House recipe. A recipe that insists upon certain fine coffees blended a special way, to bring you richer, finer, more *satisfying* coffee. No wonder Maxwell House is bought and enjoyed by more people than any other brand of coffee!

TUNE IN: *two award-winning hits—"Father Knows Best," starring Robert Young, NBC, Thursday nights, and "Mama," starring Peggy Wood, CBS-TV, Friday nights.*

Products of General Foods

Maxwell House . . . the <u>one</u> coffee with that "Good to the Last Drop" flavor!

circa 1950

it's the thought that counts

By Al Sizer, Tucson, Arizona

I learned an important lesson about giving gifts back in 1928, when I was 12 and living in Bridgeport, Connecticut. It all started as I walked into the house after finishing my paper route one day, and I overhead my mom tell a neighbor that she could really use a new garbage can.

Mom was the only one left on my shopping list, so I was happy to get a good gift idea. I went out and bought a garbage can, using money from my paper route.

I was really proud of my gift until the day before Christmas, when a friend and I were talking about our holiday shopping.

"I'm all done," I boasted, "now that I bought my mom a new garbage can."

"What?" he exclaimed in disbelief. "You're buying your mom a garbage can for Christmas? I can't believe it!"

I realized I'd made a gaffe. I wasn't old enough to understand that what people say they need isn't necessarily a good gift idea. Stores would be closing soon; how could I remedy my blunder?

Then I remembered there was a florist shop nearby that might still be open, and I still had some money left that I had planned to spend on a Christmas gift for yours truly. Instead, I ran out and bought a dozen red roses.

So that Christmas, I gave Mom a garbage can with red roses. After our family finished opening presents, I apologized to her.

"No apology necessary," she said. "It's not the gift that's important, but the love behind it. It's a lovely garbage can, and I like it as much as the roses."

After all these years, I still remember that Christmas—and always will.

Fond thoughts of first draft

In 1961, for my fifth Christmas, my paternal grandmother, Bertha Matilda Burman, sent me some new underwear. What a disappointment! Since I was beginning to learn to write, my mother said I must send a thank-you note.

I wrote, "Dear Grandma: Thank you for the underwear, but what I really wanted was a truck." I proudly showed my mom the letter. She gasped in shock and ripped it into pieces. She said I sounded ungrateful and that I should try again. That time, I simply wrote, "Thank you for the underwear."

I believed then, as I do now, that Grandma would have been delighted to get my first note. I think she would've laughed out loud, and I know that she would have sent me a truck for my birthday in February. My father would never have bought a truck for me—he believed they were only for boys. But my grandma knew that the heart wants what the heart wants.

— *Violet Finkelson, Inver Grove Heights, Minnesota*

no presents? no way!

By Elaine Leininger, Alkabo, North Dakota

I couldn't believe my ears one night when I overheard my parents saying there wouldn't be any gifts under the Christmas tree for my brother, Donald, and me. It was 1932, and we had just moved from North Dakota to Eugene, Oregon, where my parents had purchased a grocery store.

At 6, I didn't understand how the Great Depression had cost Dad his job as a grain elevator manager, forcing him to try his luck in Eugene. My parents had spent what little they'd saved to buy the store.

I slid deeper under the covers, not wanting to hear any more. What were they talking about? Of course Santa would leave something for us. He always did!

The next day, Mom broke the bad news to my brother and me: There'd be no gifts for Christmas. She explained that because we had just moved, Santa wouldn't know our address. I wouldn't accept that. I told her I'd just written a note to Santa that included our new address. I informed her that Santa would come—just wait and see!

Still, I was a little nervous about Christmas and watched to see if preparations took place as normal. So I was relieved when Dad took us kids with him to a place where he heard we could get a Christmas tree for free. We put it up at home and strung popcorn ropes and made paper chains out of the colored funny papers. It was beautiful.

Then Mom made traditional Swedish rice pudding for Christmas Day, just as she always did. Dad lit the candles on the tree, and Mom read us the Christmas story. Then they talked to us about Jesus' birthday and how we give presents to celebrate his birth. I had no doubt there'd be gifts under the tree the next morning.

Early the next day, Donald and I went to our small living room, and there were the gifts: one for him and one for me. My present was a stuffed puppy named Spare-Ribs, like the dog in the comic strip *Toots and Casper*. He was soft and cuddly, and as I wrapped my arms around him, I told Mom and Dad this was the best gift ever. I didn't understand why they had tears in their eyes when I exclaimed, "See? I told you Santa would find us!"

Years later, I learned that the American Legion provided gifts to Army veterans like my dad, who had served in World War I. So yes, Santa did come that year—in the hearts of people who give to others in need. They made a mom, a dad, a 10-year-old boy and a little girl very happy indeed.

WAIT AND SEE Author Elaine, 6, and her brother, Donald, 10, kept their holiday hopes alive, convinced Santa would have no trouble finding their new home.

Season of Giving

135

what goes around comes around

By Fannie Erickson, Arcata, California

During the Depression years in Little Rock, Arkansas, each classroom in my school was assigned a family for which we'd provide Christmas gifts and food. One memorable year, the large family we provided for had four boys and two girls, just like my family.

A friend of mine was chosen to write information about the family on the blackboard. As she wrote, I admired her flowered dress, which featured eight starched gores that flared just so.

I was assigned to get a gift for a 4-year-old girl. That was fine with me; it was better than supplying food or money for a turkey. My family had never had a turkey for Christmas; it was just another day of beans with salt pork. I didn't know what was so great about turkey, but I vowed that someday we'd find out.

I decided to donate a little sewing kit that I'd already bought for my little sister, Freda Lee, with half of the 50 cents I'd earned by helping out a neighbor. I have to admit I didn't do it willingly. But Mother talked me into it, noting that the little girl and her family might be worse off than we were.

It was hard to imagine that anyone could be worse off than our family of eight living in a one-room shack in the piney woods around Little Rock. We didn't even have an address, for goodness' sake, and Santa often missed our house.

But on the day before Christmas, I came home to see two women leaving our shack. They had just delivered a box of food and a small turkey!

On Christmas morning, another huge surprise awaited: a box of small toy cars, books, puzzles and handkerchiefs for my brothers and me. It didn't take me long to figure out the rest of it when I saw that flowered dress with eight starched gores.

Then I looked up and saw Freda Lee gleefully ripping wrapping paper off a little sewing kit labeled "female, 4 years"—written in my own handwriting! I never did find out if Mother knew the sewing kit would end up in Freda Lee's hands. But I do know it was the most amazing Christmas ever.

CHRISTMAS SURPRISE The author's donation warmed her heart and that of her younger sister, Freda Lee, both shown in front of Garland Elementary School in Little Rock, Arkansas, in 1939.

female 4 years

poetic present

By Suzi Ross Bevan, Fredericksburg, Virginia

When I was growing up in Scranton, Pennsylvania, my father started to write poems, first about me and then about everything imaginable. He'd mail them off to the *Saturday Evening Post* in hopes of getting one published, but they always came back with a kindly worded rejection letter. He had a good sense of humor; he wallpapered one wall of his office with the rejection slips. But he never stopped trying.

After my daughter was born, I wanted him to know how special his gift of poetry was to me. So in 1966, I asked him to send me a few of his favorite poems, with the pretense that I wanted to keep them for my daughter. He sent back about a dozen that were special to him.

I illustrated some of them, then had them printed in a booklet with a bright-yellow cover. I titled it *A Few Favorite Poems by Charles S. Ross Jr.* and ordered 100 copies, which I wrapped in a big box with a huge bow.

On Christmas morning, after everyone had opened their gifts, I brought out the box and put it in Dad's lap. He usually received socks or ties or handkerchiefs, so he couldn't imagine what this big, heavy box contained. As soon as he opened it and saw the booklets, the tears started flowing.

Dad could hardly speak. After much throat-clearing and wiping away of tears, he said it was the best gift he'd ever received, next to the births of his three children.

After that, he sent off many copies of the booklet to people he knew. Then he'd write to tell me where he sent them, and the recipients' reaction to the poems. The compliments he received were a thrill and blessing to him for years. I think it even made up for all those rejections from the *Post*!

RHYME AND REASON
Gathered for the family's annual Christmas picture in 1954 were (top, from left) author Suzi; her father, Charles Seabert Ross; brother Charlie; her mom, Eloise; and brother Tim. At Christmas in 1966, Suzi (above, with her parents and daughter, Michelle) had a collection of her dad's poems printed as a gift.

FAITH RESTORED Author June, left, poses in her pink knitted sweater.

family's salvation

By June Baber, Newmarket, Ontario

I was afraid Santa might forget about my family on Christmas in 1940, because we had just moved to a big house on Ontario Street in Toronto.

It was a stressful time for my family. Mom was pregnant with a baby boy who would arrive in January, and Dad was very ill in the hospital. Even at 8, I was old enough to realize it was going to be a bleak Christmas for my two sisters, Shirley and Pauline, and me. But I held out hope that Santa would find us.

When I awoke that Christmas morning, I peeked around the doorway into our living room. I could hardly believe what I saw: There wasn't a single present—not even a Christmas tree. It was so disappointing, but I tried hard not to cry.

Later that morning, someone knocked on our door. When I opened it, there stood two nice Salvation Army ladies, one of them holding a small Christmas tree. She asked if they could come in and decorate it.

They came in, put the little tree in a corner and proceeded to decorate it with red-and-green paper chains and white paper snowflakes on strings. One of the women went outside and brought back some gifts, which she then put under the tree while my sisters and I watched in wide-eyed amazement.

I still vividly recall the gifts. There was a white-hooded wicker bassinet with my name on it, and a baby doll covered by a blanket inside. I also got a navy dress with little red apples on the skirt, and a lovely pink knitted sweater. There were presents for my sisters, too.

As these dear ladies left the house, they explained that Santa had left the presents with them to bring to our home. My faith in Santa was restored—he hadn't forgotten us after all. He just wasn't sure of our new address.

That's why there will always be a soft spot in my heart for the Salvation Army and the work it does, especially around Christmas.

worth the wait

The only thing my son, Charles Griggs, wanted for Christmas
during his childhood years in Anabel, Missouri, was a little red
coaster wagon. But those were the days of the Great Depression,
when there was never any money for such an expensive toy.
But I never forgot how badly Charles wanted that wagon.
And his wish finally came true—in 1969, when he was
40 years old! It took a lot longer than I ever imagined, but I
finally gave my son his dream gift.

—*Virginia Pinkerman, Macon, Missouri*

CHAPTER EIGHT

Celebrating Overseas

Christmas was a heart-wrenching experience for many families with husbands and fathers serving overseas in the 1940s and '50s. But with can-do spirit, those families and servicemen still found ways to bring the holiday home, both here and abroad.

In 1953, for instance, Albert Bertaccini of Old Forge, Pennsylvania, kept alive the holiday spirit while stationed with the Army in Wiesbaden, West Germany. He and others in the 7th Battalion wore Santa beards and decorated a 2½-ton truck (top right) with garlands and decorations, plus signs that read, in German and English, "The Sweetest Truck in Town."

"We drove through the city, distributing bags of candy to all the children we could find," he recalls.

It was a different story for Jim Kapuscinski (bottom right) of Saginaw, Michigan, who spent two heartbreaking Christmases in Korea in 1953 and '54.

"But what a surprise when I came home in February 1955," he writes. "The family Christmas tree still stood, fully decorated with ornaments, tinsel and lights. The gifts were under the tree, wrapped in beautiful, bright paper. The only thing missing was the pine needles—they had all fallen off! I will never forget it."

For stories of other uplifting celebrations, read on.

miracle on Mindanao

By Joseph Banas
Cleveland, Ohio

My most memorable Christmas overseas was in the Philippine Islands in 1945, just after the end of World War II.

In June of that year, I had shipped out to the Philippines to join an infantry regiment on the island of Mindanao. The war was still going on when we reached our seaport destination of Cagayan de Oro, 300 miles south of Manila, where we were under constant attack from Japanese soldiers hiding up in the hills.

Thankfully, the war ended in August, and I was assigned to organize basic training for new Filipino recruits stationed at Cagayan.

Like most of the Philippines, Cagayan had been routed by the Japanese army for more than three years. The Filipinos didn't stand a chance against these ferocious and unexpected attacks. When the fighting finally stopped and the locals came down from their hiding places in the hills, they were bedraggled and worn to the bone. With no fresh water, little food and no clothing to speak of, they were living in flimsy wood or cardboard shacks.

I promised myself that before I left the islands, I would do anything I could to help these people. To keep that vow, I begged, borrowed and stole all I could get my hands on.

It wasn't long before I met a fine family by the name of Batista. The parents had been schoolteachers before the war.

Through them, I met a clergyman, Bishop Hayes, the pastor of the only remaining church in town. He'd been transferred to the islands right after the war began and was caught in the middle of the devastation. Japanese bombing blew off the entire roof of his church—the Cathedral of the Virgin Mary, named for the patron saint of the Philippines—and the roof of the parish's rectory.

The bishop was so excited to meet me that I was deeply moved—until he exclaimed,

CAN-DO SPIRIT
Army officer Joseph Banas, with a village friend in 1946 (top) and with fiancee Elly Mogyorossy in 1945 (bottom), made good on a heartfelt promise.

"Oh, Lieutenant, the good Lord promised me that you were coming and that you would help me put a roof on my church!"

Startled, I said, "Look, Bishop, I know nothing about replacing the roof of your church. The good Lord has never contacted me personally before, but I'll do whatever I can for you."

The problem was, I knew I could get my hands on just one truckload of lumber, and the bishop needed three times that amount for his church. Reluctantly, I told him it would be a miracle indeed if I could come through.

But the next morning, I contacted my colonel about the lumber I needed. Frankly, he thought I was off my rocker until I explained the bishop's urgency to him. Luckily, this good officer was also a good Catholic, and he said he'd look around for me. He knew that the

THERE IS ONE OTHER MEMORY OF MINDANAO I SHALL ALWAYS HOLD DEAR.
On a 50th-anniversary trip with my wife, Elly, I revisited the Philippines and some of the people I had come to know during the war, including members of the Batista family. One of the highlights was seeing the grand old Cathedral of the Virgin Mary, standing tall and beautiful as ever. After half a century, my miracle roof was still intact.

local citizens were mostly Catholic and that this would mean the world to them.

A few days later the colonel contacted me. "Lieutenant," he said, "I found two truckloads of old wood, but it's up in Manila. I can have it delivered to Cagayan by plane in two days, but you must have your men at the airport in time to receive it, or it will be gone quickly."

All I could say was "Aye, aye, Colonel!"

The next day we picked up the lumber and delivered it to the bishop, pronto. In turn, he contacted 50 men to work on the roof. With me scrounging up the shingles, tools and nails—thanks to the generosity of an unwitting U.S. Army—work started immediately.

Incredibly, the bishop called two days before Christmas to say that his men not only had finished both the church roof and the rectory roof, but had done all the painting and trimming inside the cathedral! Then he invited the colonel and me to join him at the midnight Mass on Christmas Eve.

When we arrived, the cathedral was beautifully decorated with candles, flowers and festive fabrics the Filipino women had hidden away during the war. It was a sight to behold. Even the bishop seemed overwhelmed.

I was profoundly grateful to have helped bring so much love and joy to the 400 people who attended this grand celebration. It was an event I will remember all my life.

YANKEE INGENUITY The author, shown here at Grace Park Airfield in Manila in 1945, made the Christmas wish of an entire Filipino village come true.

circa 1942

to Seoul with love

By John Egan, Aberdeen, Maryland

In 1952 I was with the Air Force's 6154th Air Police Squadron in Seoul, Korea. Despite the war raging around us, that Christmas turned out to be a wonderful one.

Many local people had been hired to do all types of maintenance: housekeeping, laundry, tailoring, and cutting our hair. Many of the workers brought along their children, who reminded us of our little sisters and brothers back home.

We gave special Christmas presents to the kids we had adopted as our mascots—the young son and daughter of our cleaning lady. (They also were our barber's grandchildren.)

The boy was always fascinated by our belts, guns and helmets, so we had a child-size uniform made for him. He was so proud to wear it! We gave the little girl, who always followed her big brother around, a red velvet outfit—though I can't imagine where our seamstress found velvet during the war. The kids were just delighted with their presents.

On Christmas Eve, the directors of an orphanage invited us to visit, and the children sang carols in both English and Korean. It's a memory that will always be precious to me.

FROM THE HEART John Egan (above left) and his Air Force squadron befriended the children of local workers (below left) while stationed in Seoul, Korea. They gave one boy (below center) a custom-made "Army" uniform and his sister (below right) a charming red velvet outfit.

Grandpa's twin trees

By Lois Schultz, Usk, Washington

In 1952 my husband was stationed with the Navy in Guam, and my two children and I sailed over on the *USS Barrett* to visit him. At Christmastime we received a big package from my parents. My father had gone out to our family ranch in Usk, Washington, cut a small tree and wrapped it in burlap bags to keep it fresh. My mother put in a whole bunch of small decorations for it, too. That's 4-year-old Tim (right) admiring it. What a beautiful surprise on a tropical island!

Sixteen years later, Tim went to Vietnam with the Army—sailing, believe it or not, on the *USS Barrett*! Once again, my dad came through with a long-distance Christmas tree for him. My daughter Cindy and I sent a care package with cookies, candy, toy reindeer, a Santa Claus and ornaments for the tree.

My dad, Ralph Osman, passed away in 1979, but Tim has never forgotten these amazing gifts from his grandfather.

patriotic posts

Christmas cards made the season bright for this young sailor.

By David Collier, Inverness, Florida

I joined the Navy in September 1943, when I was 17. That December, I was assigned to a ship being prepared in Tampa, Florida.

When we arrived, the ship wasn't ready, but we received a delightful Christmas surprise—a special leave home. We didn't have to report back until January.

I served in the South Pacific and during the occupation of Japan. I was discharged in May 1946.

While I was in the Navy, I received many cards from family and friends. There were cards for Christmas, birthdays and Valentine's Day.

All of the cards had a military theme and were designed for men and women in the service. I saved all of the cards, as I consider them unique and historic. I hope other readers enjoy seeing them.

▶ "May we give thanks today for the many blessings of an American Christmas."

▼ "With the Season's greetings and every good wish for happiness in the New Year."

▶ "May your ship soon sail in port with a Christmas of the finest sort."

▼ "May the true spirit of Christmas bring you peace and happiness."

bountiful blessings

By Robert Mosholder
Rio Rancho, New Mexico

At right is the menu for the Christmas dinner served to my Army unit in the Panama Canal Zone just weeks after World War II began.

Though the food was bountiful, it was a difficult Christmas. We wondered when we'd be leaving for the Pacific; some of the men had buddies serving in Hawaii and wondered if they were OK.

I was sworn in as a warrant officer in March '42 and was sent to the Pacific in May. It wasn't until 1946, while serving at Fort Bliss, Texas, that I got to celebrate Christmas the way it ought to be celebrated: with my wife, Adalene, and our newborn daughter, Sandra. What a joyous holiday season that one was! And it was matched by Christmas 1965, when our adopted infant daughter, Roberta, was in our arms.

MERRY CHRISTMAS
PANAMA

CHRISTMAS MENU
DECEMBER, 1941

Service Battery, 83rd Coast Artillery (AA)

OYSTER STEW   SODA CRACKERS
CELERY HEARTS   SWEET PICKLES   RIPE OLIVES
LETTUCE SALAD   SLICED TOMATOES
                    OYSTER COCKTAIL
                    ROAST TURKEY
SAGE DRESSING   GIBLET GRAVY
                VIRGINIA BAKED HAM
SNOWFLAKED POTATOES   CRANBERRY SAUCE
                BUTTERED ASPARAGUS
ENGLISH PEAS   CREAM CORN
            ASSORTED ROLLS AND BUTTER
CHOCOLATE CAKE   COCONUT CAKE
                    FRUIT CAKE
    PUMPKIN PIE   MINCE PIE
                MIXED CANDIES AND NUTS
    APPLES   PEARS   GRAPES   ORANGES
        ICE CREAM   COFFEE   FRUIT PUNCH
            CIGARS   CIGARETTES

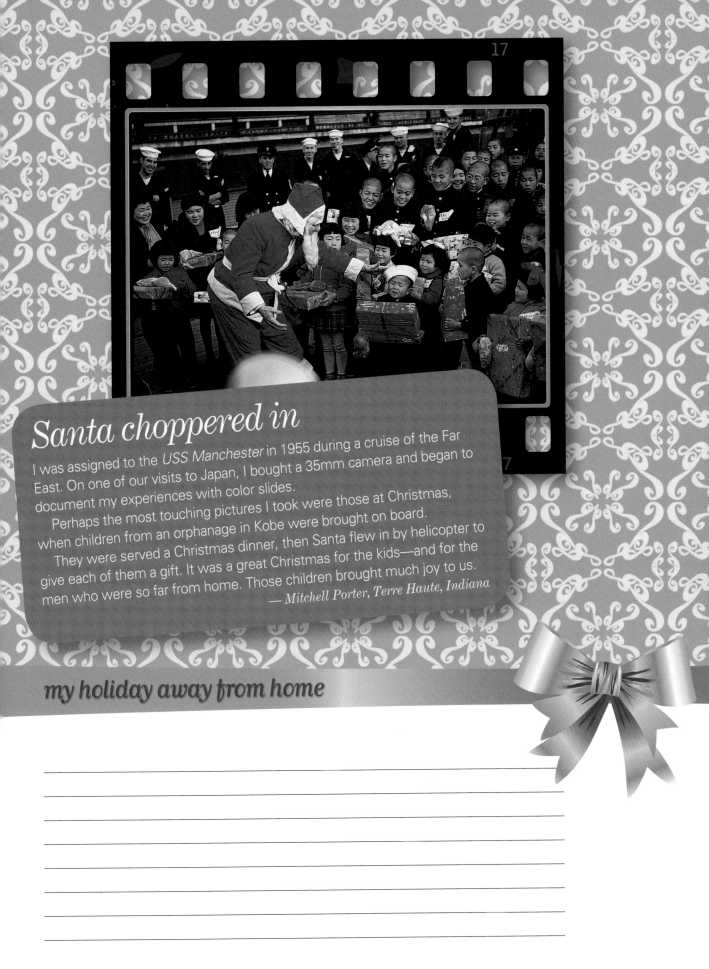

Santa choppered in

I was assigned to the *USS Manchester* in 1955 during a cruise of the Far East. On one of our visits to Japan, I bought a 35mm camera and began to document my experiences with color slides.

Perhaps the most touching pictures I took were those at Christmas, when children from an orphanage in Kobe were brought on board. They were served a Christmas dinner, then Santa flew in by helicopter to give each of them a gift. It was a great Christmas for the kids—and for the men who were so far from home. Those children brought much joy to us.
— *Mitchell Porter, Terre Haute, Indiana*

my holiday away from home

merry mischief

By A. Earl Mgebroff, Yoakum, Texas

As the holiday season of 1947 approached, my seven roommates and I from the 2nd Constabulary Regiment in occupied Germany did what we could to make our room festive.

For ornaments, we cut stars out of cardboard and wrapped them in the foil from our Hershey bars. Where, though, would we get a tree?

Then one day, looking out the window of our barracks—taken over from a German Panzer division in Augsburg—we saw a fine, tall evergreen on the sidewalk in front of the headquarters building.

After dark, we crept down for a closer look. The tree was far too big for our quarters, so we cut off the top 4 feet and quickly carted it up to our room. It made one of the prettiest Christmas trees I've ever seen.

We heard later that the tree had been procured for Col. Elms, who was quite upset to find only the bottom of it remaining. Fortunately for us, he didn't pursue the mysterious disappearance of the top.

We also made our own Christmas cards by taking comic photos of ourselves as carolers and various other characters.

Our band director, Warrant Officer Heinzel, was assisted by a former German military band director, a congenial man we all liked very much. On Christmas Eve, we visited him and his family, bringing gifts for the children and taking some Hershey bars along with us. Chocolate was precious to the local people, who had little but the bare necessities after the war.

That holiday season, our mess sergeant found out the nuns were raiding our garbage cans at night to get food for the children at their orphanage. So he made a new rule. We were to take what we wanted, but only as much as we could eat. Less waste would mean we could donate fresh food to the orphanage. The lesson sank in. To this day, it feels wrong to me to leave food on my plate.

Though we were far from home and missed our loved ones, Christmas 1947 turned out to be a blessing.

And to Col. Elms: Please forgive us, wherever you are.

SPIRITED SOLDIERS Earl Mgebroff and soldiers from his regiment decorated a pilfered tree *(right)* and created Christmas cards of carolers *(below)*.

"Look, Bob—an Elgin from the folks!"

In the islands of the Pacific . . . in England . . . on ships at sea . . . this will be a "box-from-home" Christmas for many a fighting Yank.

Call it tradition, if you wish. Call it sentiment. But if the gifts you have sent include an Elgin watch, then it's bound to be a real American Christmas!

Yes, for the member of your family doing a job on the fighting front or home front, an Elgin is the perfect remembrance.

Of course, fewer of these watches are available this year, due to Elgin's war effort. Long before Pearl Harbor even, the government requested Elgin to produce special military devices and precision instruments. And these today are Elgin's first concern. Fighting planes, tanks and guns must be equipped.

However, each one of the Elgins your jeweler is offering is star-timed and true to the famous Elgin standard of dependability. Each is produced by Elgin's unique partnership of fourth-generation craftsmen and scientists.

You will also be interested in your jeweler's many other fine gifts of quality, including exquisite precious and semi-precious stones and silverware. *A gift means so much when it comes from your jeweler's.*

(Top) *Elgin Service Watch. Luminous dial. Sweep hand.*
(Bottom) *Thin Lord Elgin. 14K natural gold filled case.*

Brilliantly designed Lady Elgin. 14K rosé gold filled.

ELGIN

*Since 1865 a great
American gift tradition*

Beautiful Elgin De Luxe. Star-timed for superb accuracy.

HOPES SING ETERNAL Claire Kirk (left) and her sisters, Anne and Terese, sang as the Hope Sisters, entertaining troops in the Pacific and making Christmas of 1944 special.

songs from on high

By Claire Kirk, Belgrade, Maine

Memories of joyous holidays with the big family of my childhood will last forever—but there was one very different Christmas that my sisters, Anne and Terese, and I have always cherished.

As young ladies of 19, 20 and 21, we performed professionally as the Hope Sisters, appearing in clubs, theaters and veterans hospitals all over the country. While singing in Los Angeles in 1943, we were asked to go overseas with the USO. We agreed, were commissioned as lieutenant commanders with the Navy, and were sent to the Pacific, where we sang for the troops on Saipan, Iwo Jima and many other islands.

On Christmas Eve 1944, we found ourselves performing in Guam. After finishing our last show, my sisters and I headed back to our Quonset hut, which sat on a hill.

We talked about what we'd be doing if we were back home. Most of the talk was cheerful, but it was hard to be so far from home.

Down below us were the quarters for the servicemen. As darkness fell, we saw lights going out as the men got ready to retire. Our hearts ached at the loneliness those boys must have felt.

Suddenly, one of us began humming *Silent Night*. Before we knew it, all three of us were harmonizing in the dark.

Down below us, lights flickered back on until the whole compound was lit up. Under the clear starry sky, men quietly came out of their huts. At first, they just listened—but then, in the distance, we heard their voices joining us in singing carols. The moment was beautiful.

When we finally stopped singing that night, we saw many of the men shaking hands or embracing in friendship. Then they waved to us, and we heard a resounding "Thank you! Merry Christmas!" make its way up the hill.

Although we'd been feeling a little low just moments before, we now felt joyful. It's a poignant memory I will keep forever.

peace was best gift

In 1955, while serving with the 9th Marine Regiment on Okinawa,
I received this tree from my family in Eureka, California. Even though
the box was crushed, the tree itself—and the handmade ornaments
to decorate it—had made it across the Pacific in excellent condition.
Many of us had served through World War II and Korea
and would later go to Vietnam. But this Christmas was special:
There was peace, so we took time to enjoy the tree, sing carols
and give thought to what Christmas was really all about.

— *James Morrow, San Juan Capistrano, California*

CHAPTER NINE

Magic of the Season

Each Christmas season is filled with opportunities to experience magic and wonder—from the awe a child feels first meeting the jolly old elf himself to the joy of finding a longed-for toy under the tree early on Christmas morning.

But sometimes one particular Christmas rises above the others, like the 1961 classic that still vividly evokes fond memories for Sharon Rawlings Provence of Granite City, Illinois.

"I was 6 years old and my sister, Brenda, was 8," she recalls. "I remember going to downtown Granite City to Santa's Cabin to tell Santa that I wanted a Tiny Tears doll.

"After visiting Santa (at right), we walked through gently falling snow to Woolworth's. What fun store to visit at Christmas!

"Then we went home and baked sugar cookies, cut in shapes like bells, stars and the baby Jesus. Then, a week before Christmas, we went back downtown to buy a Christmas tree.

"After decorating it, Brenda and I liked to lie under the tree and laugh at our reflections in those mirrorlike ball ornaments. These memories with my sister, dad, Gerald, and mom, Jean (bottom right), feel as if they just happened yesterday."

Read on, and enjoy more magical stories of the season like these.

secret wish granted

By Hiroko Plummer, West Hills, California

It may seem odd, but my most memorable Christmas came during the most difficult time for my family—a period of intense hardship that followed a dispiriting three years in a Japanese-American internment camp in Manzanar, California.

When the camps disbanded after World War II, my mother and father had to start all over again in two drab, hulking trailer homes in Sun Valley, with six children and nothing more than two large footlockers that contained all the possessions we owned.

We were among about 40 Japanese families who banded together to work and re-establish meaningful lives. Our camp consisted of nothing more than shabby, oppressive trailers that had once housed construction workers who built the Hoover Dam on the Arizona-Nevada border. The trailers had no heat or plumbing, so we used public restrooms and showers. They leaked whenever it rained, and the cold drafts that whistled through the cracks made life miserable in winter. We wished summer would never end!

After about eight years of hard work, scrimping and saving, the camp disbanded as the families bought or built homes and began to enter mainstream society. But the trailer-camp years were tough times for us all, and Christmas was no different.

Each of us children usually received one inexpensive toy, something we had wanted badly throughout the year. When I was 5, I wanted a toy accordion, which I'd seen many times in the window at Woolworth's. I was thrilled to receive it on Christmas morning, though I knew it was from my parents, not Santa. The gift from Santa was always a stocking full of sticky hard candy with a quarter buried down at the toe.

When I was 6, I really wanted a doll and buggy for Christmas, along with a set of blue dishes with tiny flowers around the edges. I knew my parents couldn't afford these gifts, but I thought Santa would surely bring them if

RARE REQUEST Hiroko (left) asked for special gifts from Santa. She was about 6 in this photo taken in 1947 or 1948 with sister Sachi (in front) and a friend.

he only knew how desperately I wanted them.

So I decided to write a letter to Santa. I didn't want my parents or brothers and sisters to know about the letter, for fear they'd get mad or think it was silly. My parents were proud people who believed

Today, I marvel at their kindness—and how courageous they were to come to our camp when only a few years before we were considered an enemy people.

in earning things by working for them, not asking for them.

I wasn't old enough to write a letter, so my 9-year-old friend Evelyn helped me. She sat on the steps of her family's trailer and patiently wrote while I dictated. At the end of the letter, I implored Santa, "Please, please, please bring it to me this Christmas!"

We addressed the letter to Santa Claus, North Pole, and dropped it in the mailbox that served our trailer camp. None of the trailers had addresses; there was just one mailing address for the entire camp. We lived on the farthest edge of the camp, and non-Japanese visitors were rare.

Several weeks later, I heard two older boys shouting my name. They said two people were looking for me, and by the ominous tone of their voices, I thought it must be the police. Even though I couldn't recall doing anything terrible, I panicked and ran to one of our trailers, where I hid in a closet.

But my older brother found me and dragged me outside to face the visitors: a thin, wiry man and a neatly dressed woman standing next to a cream-colored Chevy. The gentle-faced man calmed me down by explaining that because Santa was going to be so busy on Christmas Eve, he'd enlisted some helpers to make a few early deliveries.

Then the woman opened the car door and slowly took out a doll, a buggy and a set of blue dishes. I was overjoyed! I knew Santa wouldn't fail me! Then they handed my brother a newspaper, where the letter Evelyn had so laboriously written for me was on the front page. I thanked them and they drove away.

Later, I learned that these "Santa's helpers" were really two postal workers who'd bought the gifts with their own money. Today, I marvel at their kindness—and how courageous they were to come to our camp when only a few years before we were considered an enemy people.

That was more than 60 years ago, and to this day I still think about those two generous people every Christmas. I've received many gifts since then, but none meant more to me than that doll, buggy and dish set!

my most magical Christmas moment

_____

_____

_____

_____

_____

sleigh bell surprise

By Dick Pratt, Chester, Vermont

One Christmas Eve in the early 1930s, back when I was 4 or 5 years old, I was playing with toys when I heard sleigh bells. The sound came closer, then went around the corner of our house. I ran to the window but couldn't see a thing, as it was as black as ink outside.

As I ran into our kitchen, I heard the sound of the bells coming from our woodshed—presumably, I reasoned, so Santa could feed his reindeer some of our grain. I sprinted to the kitchen door that led to the woodshed and flung it open. What I saw was totally unexpected: my uncle Bill dangling a set of sleigh bells in one hand and wearing a sheepish grin on his face.

I ran over to him and embraced one of his legs. Then Ma appeared behind me, looking pretty angry. Uncle Bill swooped me up in his big arms and hugged and kissed me, then handed me the bells, saying, "Hi, li'l Richard. I tried to catch Santa for you, but all I got were the bells off the reindeer as they flew by!"

I just grinned, hugged and kissed him and ran back into the house, happily jingling the bells. In the background, I could hear Ma giving him a piece of her mind. I couldn't figure out why, as I thought he'd done a good job just getting the bells off the speeding reindeer. It couldn't have upset Santa too much, for the next day, there were presents under the tree for everyone.

Many years later, Uncle Bill died of a sudden heart attack at age 89. As I sat at the funeral, listening to the minister, I saw my uncle in my mind's eye, standing in a barn so many, many years ago, Santa's sleigh bells dangling from his hand. He must've loved his little nephew an awful lot to try to outrun Santa's reindeer.

an evergreen miracle

By Doris Lindley, Avon, Connecticut

One snowy Christmas Eve, my two sisters and I couldn't wait for our father to come home from work so we could go out and buy a Christmas tree. When he arrived, he got out our Flexible Flyer sled, on which he'd built a box to hold the three of us. He piled us inside and began to pull us down the snow-covered sidewalk. In no time, our cheeks stung from the cold, but we didn't mind, so great was our anticipation.

We finally reached an avenue lined with men selling evergreens. My father went from vendor to vendor, offering them one dollar for a tree. One by one, they chuckled and declined his offer. Soon it got dark enough for the streetlights to turn on, which made the falling snowflakes look magical. But we were getting cold and scared; we were almost down to the last vendor, and still no tree. A Christmas without a tree where Santa could place gifts was a frightening thought.

But the last vendor agreed to take a dollar for a skinny, scraggly tree, which Daddy proudly tied to the side of the sled. He ran all the way home, pulling us behind as we sang Christmas carols and caught snowflakes on our tongues.

> ## She trimmed and turned, yanked and pulled, then at last stepped back to take a look. It was a perfect Christmas tree!

When we got home, Dad cut off the bottom of the tree so it would fit in the stand without hitting the ceiling. Then he set it up—and we realized it was missing many branches and seemed way too skinny to decorate. But Daddy patted our backs and said we shouldn't worry; the branches would fall down and fill in as the tree warmed up. With that, he settled into his easy chair and was asleep within seconds.

That's when Mommy appeared, armed with an electric drill and an extension cord. Without a word, she went to work, drilling holes in the trunk by the bare spots and filling them with branches she removed from fuller parts of the tree. She trimmed and turned, yanked and pulled, then at last stepped back to take a look. It was a perfect Christmas tree!

Our squeals of delight woke Dad up, so he went to the attic to get the decorations. As he walked up the stairs, we could hear him say, "I told you girls it would be a perfect Christmas tree after it warmed up."

We learned that sometimes perfect takes a little help. But with a little faith, miracles do happen!

cherished photo

By Bonnie Baker Leuser, Ancaster, Ontario

With a toddler and prematurely born triplets, my mother was pretty much housebound during our early years. The triplets—Allan, Barbara and I—joined our brother, Glenn, who was 2, in February 1951.

Our physician was so unsure of our prognosis that he snapped black-and-white photos of each of us in our special cribs and our oxygen masks. The photos were meant be a reminder for Mum and Dad in case we didn't survive.

But our condition improved as we grew older. And as Christmas neared in 1952, Mum did something totally uncharacteristic, perhaps prompted by some strong maternal instinct. She decided to take all four of us to see Santa—without a car or any help from family. This was no small feat, as she had to push a custom-built triple stroller through snow and cold in order to take a bus into town.

At the bus stop, a kind bus driver got out to help her. Mum handed each of us off to the driver, who in turn found passengers to hold us while he collapsed the stroller and loaded it on board.

THREE OF A KIND Triplets Barbara, left, Bonnie and Allan Baker were 22 months old when this picture was taken with Santa.

The next hurdle was at Robinson's department store, where the stroller was too wide to fit through the door. Someone alerted the store manager, who loaded us into a freight elevator to take us up to Toyland. As she stood in line, Mum removed our homemade snowsuits for our photo with Santa. She had made identical overall outfits for the three of us; she made all our clothes, assembly-line style, in multiples of three.

Mom's mission was exhausting. But she was forever thankful that she made the extra effort, because at age 2, Allan's health began to deteriorate, and 10 months later he became our guardian angel. We, too, were grateful for her resolve. We still prominently display the photo of the three of us together that Christmas season. It always reminds us of Allan—and of Mum's steadfast resolve to create a cherished Christmas memory for us all.

treasured gifts

By Lora Devereaux, Carson City, Nevada

During Christmas 1966, my dad was stationed in Japan with the U.S. Marine Corps. I was 6, and I really missed my daddy. I didn't understand what "overseas" meant. All I knew was that before he was shipped out, we moved to Long Beach, California, to live near my grandparents.

On Christmas Eve, my mother, sister and I went to my grandparents' house for dinner. Later that night, my grandpa must have snuck out and driven to our apartment to arrange things. After dinner, we drove back home with my grandparents. As we walked into our apartment, my mother flipped on the lights, and much to my surprise, there were Christmas presents everywhere! My sister and I didn't know what to think; we certainly didn't understand where they all came from.

There were dolls and tea sets, doll furniture, books, stuffed animals, a child-size table and chairs, clothes and boxes of books. It was overwhelming. To my 6-year-old eyes, it looked like a fairyland. We opened up package after package while Mom and Grandma took pictures. Years later, I learned that many of our relatives sent presents because they felt so sorry that Dad couldn't be home for Christmas.

But the most wonderful present of all was a beautiful grown-up black-lacquered jewelry box that Dad shipped home just for me. He also sent my mother a bottle of her favorite perfume, Chanel No. 5.

I remember opening the package that held the jewelry box and feeling such awe as I opened the lid and listened to the music. I was so thankful to receive such a special present. I still have the jewelry box today—as well as cherished memories of wonderful relatives who made Christmas special for two little girls who dearly missed their daddy.

SPECIAL SURPRISE
Child-sized furniture (left) and packages piled around the tree (bottom left) brightened Christmas Eve 1966 for Lora Deveraux. Particularly meaningful were gifts from her dad stationed overseas: a jewelry box for her (far left) and perfume for Mom (below).

circa 1951

a visit from Mrs. Claus

By Jim Stamberger, Independence, Missouri

In December 1964, we lived in a crumbling bungalow in Independence, Missouri. A color wheel lit our living room and brightened our aluminum Christmas tree. But that pretty sight contrasted with the worry my parents always felt at Christmas. The meager salary my father earned as a janitor at the First Baptist Church barely covered our normal living expenses. It was especially difficult for my mother, who wanted a good Christmas for her boys. We always received presents, but my mother fretted nonetheless.

One night, we were watching *Rudolph, the Red-Nosed Reindeer* on our black-and-white TV. Expectation hung in the air, and during the commercials my brother and I talked about what we wanted. But my mother kept reminding us Christmas would be lean because parents had to help Santa with the cost of toys.

Then it happened. We heard a knock at the door, and there she was—Mrs. Claus herself. She had her white hair up in a bun, wore a red-and-green gingham dress with a ruffled apron, and smelled like Christmas cookies.

She said she came to remind us that Santa was busy loading his sleigh with toys. Meanwhile, she was checking on children to make certain that they believed in the jolly man in the red coat, and that they were being good little boys and girls.

> *We heard a knock at the door, and there she was—Mrs. Claus herself. She had her white hair up in a bun, wore a red-and-green gingham dress with a ruffled apron, and smelled like Christmas cookies.*

While I assured her we did believe and were trying to be good, my little brother hid behind Mama, clutching at the hem of her housedress. Then that sweet little lady set off, but not before giving us each a small piece of candy— and a memory to cherish for many years.

I was in awe. It changed the whole night and the whole season; it made Santa seem so real and so close. That was the first time I experienced what people mean when they talk about the magic of the season.

Years later, I asked my mother if she knew who Mrs. Claus really was. She replied that no one seemed to know. This seemed impossible, as my mother and the other neighborhood women seemed to know everything that went on in our little world.

We figured she must have simply been a woman who spent an evening passing out candy and a little Christmas cheer.

But to this day, I swear my brother and I met Mrs. Claus on that enchanted night. Wherever you are, Mrs. Claus, this 50-year-old man still believes—and I'm still trying to be a good little boy.

picture-perfect paper dolls

This enchanting photo was taken in 1936 after the Christmas program at the Salt Creek country school, west of Hutchinson, Kansas. I was one of the school's eight students, and the program's theme was paper dolls. The "Paper Doll Girls" shown here performed a short play for friends and family. Our mothers made muslin dresses, sewed crepe paper on them and painted the edges of the paper gold. They also made matching bonnets. Everyone thought we were so cute, they took us to a photography studio in town to have this picture taken. Shown from left are my cousin Shirley White, 5; Virginia Dean; Ramona Neuenschwander; my sister, Donna White, 7; Dorothy Scott; and me, then Delpha White, 6. The picture was hand-tinted to show the pretty colors of our dresses.

— *Delpha Engelland, Hutchinson, Kansas*

yes, Virginia, there is a Santa Claus

Few things make Christmas more magical than a child's heartfelt belief in the jolly man in the red suit who delivers toys to good girls and boys. And parents often go to great lengths to perpetuate the pure innocence of that fervent belief—if only for one more year.

Here are some poignant tales from *Reminisce* readers about parents who valiantly labored to keep their children's belief in Santa alive, and in doing so made lifelong memories that keep the holiday spirit burning bright.

Santa knows all—scout's honor!

More than 40 years ago, our family was involved in Cub Scouts and would faithfully attend pack meetings, so we got to know many of the boys who were in our older sons' classes.

One day close to Christmas, I took our youngest son, Jim, who was about 4, to Hennessy's department store in Helena, Montana, to see Santa Claus. Santa went through the usual questions, asking Jim if he'd been a good boy all year and what he wanted for Christmas. After Jim responded, Santa started asking Jim about his brothers, Tom and Bruce!

The look on Jim's face was priceless. Santa really knew his brothers? Amazing! I took a closer look and realized Santa was one of the older boys who'd been a classmate and fellow Cub Scout of our older sons. I smiled at Santa to show I'd recognized him. And you'd better believe Jim was a true believer in Santa Claus!

—*Olga Campbell, Bozeman, Montana*

I swear it was Santa

On Christmas Eve 1953, my 6-year-old brother, Butchie, and I vowed to stay awake, in shifts if necessary, to see Santa Claus in person. I was 8 and had just read *A Visit from St. Nicholas* to him, and we were sure that we, too, could catch Santa in the act and maybe shake his hand or get an autograph.

That Christmas, we asked for a swing and slide set from the Sears, Roebuck store in Tyler, Texas. As we listened for Santa, we heard a noise out in the backyard. We opened the window to hear what must be a welcoming party for the jolly old elf himself. It went on for hours, and we finally fell asleep without catching him under our tree.

The next morning we realized that the noise must have been old St. Nick and his helpers putting up our swing set. At breakfast, Butchie was solemn. He took a deep breath and said to the family, "I need to tell you something. Santa Claus cusses. Bad." —*Claudia Jurney, Dover, Arkansas*

merry mishap

Following Santa's footprints

As a child growing up in the 1940s, I recall there was always a lot of snow near Christmas. My dad told us Santa peeked in our windows to make sure we were behaving, so every morning we'd look out the dining room window to see if he'd been there.

Whenever there was snow, sure enough, we'd see footprints that came up to the window—but none going away. How did Santa do that? We could never figure that out as kids, but now I know that Dad would walk backward in his own footprints to create that illusion for us.

I'm now in my 70s, and I still cry whenever I think about how Dad loved us so much that he'd make time to do this before leaving for work on those snowy mornings.

—*Mary Ann Carp, Hampton, Georgia*

Good to go for one more year

When we lived in Jenkintown, Pennsylvania, many years ago, we taught our children that the real Santa Claus was the one at Wanamaker's department store in Philadelphia—all the rest were just helpers. Every holiday season, we'd take the children for dinner at Wanamaker's crystal dining room, then visit Santa.

At the time, my husband, Chuck, knew the retired gentleman who played Santa there. As we stood and watched our children walk up to Santa (above right), Chuck motioned

BELIEVERS Ray, Barbie and Shirley Ann had no doubts after Santa greeted them as "the little Woodson children" in '55.

to his friend that these were our kids. Santa picked up our youngest daughter, sat her on his lap and asked, "How are the little Woodson children from Jenkintown today?" Our oldest daughter, who was starting to become very skeptical of the whole Santa story, was a believer for another year!

—*Charlotte Woodson, Lebanon, Ohio*

Stoked about Santa

My grandparents owned a building with a coal furnace. Each night, someone had to check the fire and bank it. One Christmas Eve when I was a little girl, that chore fell to my great-uncle Jule.

I was looking out the window when I dimly saw a man walk by, carrying a sack. When he saw me, he bent over and tossed the sack over his shoulder. I was so excited; I knew I had just seen Santa Claus! My parents could hardly get me to bed. After 98 Christmas Eves, I still remember the one when I saw Santa with his sack full of toys. —*Lorene Sedlacek St. Paul, Minnesota*

my first encounter with Santa

_____

_____

_____

_____

_____

_____

Magic of the Season

impromptu invite

By Carol Clark Garrett, Pewaukee, Wisconsin

The Christmas of 1954 was easily the most magical of all the ones our family celebrated together. I was 12, and my sister, Sharon, was 14. We lived in Sioux City, Iowa, where our charismatic father, Gene Clark, was district sales manager for Air-Way Sanitizer, the best vacuum cleaner of the day.

He and my mother, Lowie, decided to host an afternoon Christmas party for the salesmen who worked for Dad and their families. We spent hours cleaning, putting up the Christmas tree, covering every square inch of the house with decorations and doing a huge amount of cooking and baking.

The night before the party, we went to bed, hardly able to sleep because we were so excited. But when we woke up, we discovered that a snowstorm had been raging all night, and there was no end in sight. Our parents spoke on the phone with the guests, and because they lived in outlying areas, they felt it was too dangerous to travel to our home. So there we sat, with a house ready for a grand party and disappointment beyond belief.

Unwilling to waste such a great celebration or to deal with moping, Dad called the local orphanage and asked if they wanted to bring some children to our party. He promised them fun, food and toys. He explained that we had all this wonderful food that wouldn't keep, plus toys we had purchased for the salesmen's children—even providing details on the number of toys and age ranges, so they could be matched with the appropriate children.

That afternoon, adults and maybe seven or eight children from the orphanage arrived at our home. We had an incredible amount of fun eating, singing and playing games with the children. Santa Claus—a neighbor my parents had arranged to appear at the original party—even came and passed out gifts to all!

What could have been a disappointment turned into one of my greatest holiday memories, thanks to my parents' quick thinking and kind, generous hearts. I hope the wonderful people we celebrated with have as fond memories of that night as I do.

KIND HEARTS Carol, her father, Gene, and sister, Sharon (far left), along with her mom, Lowie (far right), welcomed children from a local orphanage into their home to celebrate with Santa (center).

thrilled but tongue-tied

By Esther Daniels, Poulsbo, Washington

In 1945, when I was 6, my mother took me to see Santa Claus at the Frederick & Nelson department store in downtown Seattle. It was a very large building with plate-glass windows around the ground floor. Behind the windows were display areas that were beautifully decorated during the Christmas season.

Santa sat behind one special window equipped with a door to the outside. Children and their parents waited in line along the sidewalk outside until it was time to come through the door and talk to him. As you can see in the photo (right), Santa's microphone let everyone waiting outside hear what was being said.

I was so thrilled to be there, as I had never seen Santa in person. Mom told me many, many years later that I wanted just two things: a coat with a belt and a bicycle with a bell. But I was so excited when my turn came that I asked Santa for "a coat with a bell and a bicycle with a belt"!

I was almost as thrilled when the picture arrived in the mail. I cherish it because it was the one and only time that I visited Santa, and because my mother did so much to make it a special day. The war had just ended, and I think she felt I needed something special.

HE UNDERSTANDS Excitement got the best of little Esther Daniels in 1945 during her one and only visit with Santa.

in the nick of time

By Marion Holmes, Whitesboro, New York

My parents always managed to give us a happy Christmas with good food, overflowing stockings, a nice tree and gifts. But during the Depression, it looked as though they wouldn't be able to afford much of anything. In November, they came up with a dramatic solution: cashing in a small insurance policy.

As the oldest child at age 11, I no longer believed in Santa. But I joined my parents in carefully preserving the myth for my 9-year-old sister, Betty, and 7-year-old brother, Bobby, both unaware of the financial drama unfolding in our house.

After my parents sent in the insurance policy in November, we began a mailbox vigil. In those days, mail came twice a day, so Mom and I would check the mailbox twice. But day after day, there was no check to be found.

Our dreams of a Christmas celebration dwindled. Bobby wanted a small pool table and Betty wanted a Kitty Joy doll, and they both were sure Santa wouldn't let them down. He'd always come through before. I dreamed about new roller skates but knew that without the insurance check, that was impossible—they cost $2.98.

Dec. 21, 22 and 23 came and went without a check. But on the morning of Dec. 24, the mailman delivered a brown envelope. I snatched up the precious missive, read the return address and ran into the house, calling for Mom as I leapt up the stairs two at a time. Thrilled, she put the check in her pocketbook before we headed out to shop. To save the 10-cent bus fare, we walked downtown, where I helped pick out the pool table, the doll and the skates, then walked home laden with all our packages.

Christmas Day dawned warm and beautiful. After joyously opening gifts, going to church and enjoying a Christmas dinner, I headed outside to roller-skate with my friends and cousins. When we finished, we trooped into the house to play pool and eat Christmas candy and nuts. No millionaire, we all agreed, ever had a finer holiday.

WATCHFUL EYE Marion Tanner (left) monitored the mailbox until a check arrived to pay for Christmas gifts for herself and her siblings, Bob and Betty.

by the chimney with care

In 1949, my husband, Art, and I saved our money and purchased
a 35mm Kodak camera as our Christmas present to each other.
We have many slides taken over the years that capture special moments
in our children's lives. This one from 1955 shows our youngest son, Bob,
who was 3 at the time, taking the first peek into his Christmas stocking.

— *Louella Kightlinger, Erie, Pennsylvania*

holiday mystery

By Sharon Foley, Loveland, Colorado

In the spring of 1946, our family moved from Salt Lake City to rural Orem, Utah, where my parents had purchased a rundown 10-acre farm that included a ramshackle house. I was 7 and my sister, LaWana, was 8.

Dad, a carpenter by trade, set out to make the home livable. While he gutted the house that summer, we lived in a tent, eating meals picnic-style and bathing in an old washtub. Before the first snowfall, we moved into a combination bedroom and living area in the basement while Dad kept working upstairs.

When Thanksgiving rolled around, LaWana and I started thinking about Christmas. We wondered where Mom and Dad would put a tree. It couldn't be in the basement, and the rest of the house was mainly a construction zone—including a blocked-off living room.

The mystery deepened the week before Christmas when Mom and Dad kept making furtive trips into the blockaded living room. We kept pestering them about a tree and wondered how Santa would ever find us in the basement. To make it worse, we didn't see them bringing in any wrapped packages, either.

"Maybe they've forgotten about Christmas altogether," I whispered to LaWana one wintry night as we snuggled together in our bed.

Christmas Eve arrived, and still no tree or gifts. We went to bed disappointed and wondered what to expect the next morning. We'd asked for dolls and velvet dresses, which we hoped to find under a tree. But there was no tree in our house.

On Christmas morning, Mom and Dad woke us up early. Dad gathered us in his arms and carried us upstairs—and into the newly renovated living room. There in the middle of the room stood the most beautiful Christmas tree we'd ever seen. We squealed with delight and danced around the glowing tree. Under it, we found beautiful dolls and velvet dresses.

My sister and I joyfully hugged each other and agreed that this was truly a Christmas miracle never to be forgotten.

NO CHRISTMAS? The Lupus home (bottom left) was under renovation at Christmastime in 1946, making sisters LaWana (below, left) and Sharon fear the worst.

our amazing mom

By Carolyn Hood, New Freedom, Pennsylvania

When we look through family photo albums, we always chuckle when we see the Christmas photo from 1948. We kiddingly refer to this holiday as the "Charlie Brown Christmas," a reference to the scraggly little tree shown in the background.

Mother good-naturedly accepted our joshing over the years, but one day she told us the real story behind the picture. That year, our baby sister, Margaret, was born on Dec. 15. Daddy had just come home from the hospital after nearly dying from a blood clot after surgery. So Mother, even though she had just given birth, was very busy taking care of a new baby, four older children and my father.

Despite having no time for herself, she was determined that Christmas not disappoint us. In addition to presents, Mother made sure we had a Christmas tree. On Christmas Eve, she walked to the corner tree lot (she did not drive), and I believe she paid 25 cents for the last tree on the lot. Then she carried the tree home, managed to get it into the stand and decorated it before we kids woke up.

On Christmas morning, Mother dressed up in stockings and high heels with her hair curled, and all of us kids were dressed nicely, too. Daddy took this picture—minus our baby sister, who was asleep in a cradle.

We weren't showered with presents, but we were always delighted with what we received, as well as thankful for a strong mother who made sure Christmas would be special no matter what the circumstances.

STRONG SPIRIT
Hazel Russell (seated) single-handedly made Christmas 1948 bright for children Darrell, 4, Carolyn, 2, Peggy, 7, and Nina, 9. Not pictured is baby Margaret, asleep in her cradle.

what a doll!

By Ralph Pippert, Brandon, Manitoba

VIGILANCE REWARDED While a high school teacher in the 1950s, Ralph Pippert waited patiently during the weeks leading up to Christmas for the price to drop on dolls for his young daughters (above).

When my two daughters were about 5 and 6, I walked with them through stores to get gift ideas for Christmas. What really caught their eyes were two blue-eyed, pink-cheeked dolls, each wearing a blue dress. The dolls were almost as large as my daughters.

I cringed, because at $8 each, the dolls cost way too much for a teacher's salary in the 1950s. I tried to explain to the girls that Santa Claus had many children to provide for, and that every child didn't always get exactly what she wanted. It was a feeble attempt to make myself feel better, though I don't think it did anything for them.

In the following weeks, we often walked by those dolls, the girls stopping and casting envious stares. In the final days before Christmas, I checked on those dolls almost every day. In those days, stores tended to drop the prices of items that didn't sell as the holiday neared. I hoped for a discount—and that they'd still be available.

A few days before Christmas, the price dropped to $6—still out of my price range. The next day, they were marked down to $4 each, but even that was too much: You could buy a family's meat for a month with that much money.

The morning of Christmas Eve, the dolls were still marked $4 each. But at a scant 10 minutes before closing time, they still weren't sold—and were suddenly marked down to $2 each! I quickly bought them, using my last $5.

The memory of my girls' shouts of joy when they saw those dolls under the tree on Christmas morning still brings tears to my eyes. The dolls are long gone, but the happiness I felt at being able to bring them home still touches my heart today.

Christmas Time is Toy Time
Give American Toys

FOR THE BEST Christmas of all give American toys! American toys are designed first for fun, of course, and for safety; they're made in factories that meet rigid American sanitary standards.

And besides bringing long lasting joy, American toys are planned to help children discover their aptitudes—to prepare for their future careers. American toys are an important investment in education and are scientifically designed to fit children's needs at each age level.

This year American toy manufacturers bring you a record selection of thrilling new toys and new versions of old favorites at prices to fit all budgets.

So when you shop for children, go to your favorite toy department or toy store and ask to see the latest American toys. That's the one sure way to make this Christmas the best Christmas of all.

The American Toy Institute

200 FIFTH AVENUE, NEW YORK CITY 10

circa 1950

the perfect prize

By Florine Cherwin, Milwaukee, Wisconsin

During the days when skill contests, as opposed to sweepstakes, were popular, some of my friends called me a contest junkie.

I'd won a few items, including a refrigerator, so when General Mills sponsored a contest with a first prize of $10,000, I was hooked.

The contest was to name the three cartoon characters on the Cocoa Puffs cereal box: a boy, a girl and a cocoa-colored character. I bought a box of the cereal and tossed a few Puffs on the kitchen counter for inspiration.

I finally decided on something simple: Bubbles for the girl, Bouncy for the boy and Brownie for the little character. My mind was out of cutesy names, so these would just have to do. I filled out the form and sent it in.

Christmas was approaching, and I knew my son wanted an electric train, but the budget couldn't be stretched. If I won, I knew where some of that $10,000 would go.

I finally heard back from the contest. "Congratulations!" said the letter. "You are a winner"—I already saw myself at the bank with that $10,000 check—"of second prize"—oh, well, easy come, easy go—"a Lionel train set!"

The train arrived the first week in December, complete with a landscaped 4-by-6-foot plywood layout. There was even a red fire hydrant with a dog that ran around it at the touch of a switch. It was sheer magic!

what would Daddy say?

This is a Christmas card we made with the help of my husband's uncle Fred, an amateur photographer. It was taken in 1952 when our daughter, Susan, was 3 and son, Dana, was 2. The expressions on their faces show how really astonished they were to see "Mommy kissing Santa Claus"— my husband, Jack. This was around the time the song was so popular.

— *Barbara Larson, Franklin, Massachusetts*

CHAPTER TEN

A Time for Toys

Who can ever forget waking up on Christmas morning, giddy with excitement and eager to see if Santa Claus came through with that long-awaited coaster wagon, a beautiful, rosy-cheeked doll or a bright-red fire truck?

For sheer, unabashed glee, it's tough to top the reaction of 6-year-old Bonni Bauer (now Bonni Rice) after Santa delivered a Royal Racer sled in 1950 (top right). "It snowed on Christmas Eve, so she was really happy—as you can tell from her delighted grin!" recalls her mother, Irma Bauer Foster, of Chesterton, Indiana.

"In our eyes, the best Christmas ever for my brother Greg, sister Jacki and me came in 1954, when we lived in Prescott, Arizona," writes Judy Elsner of North Springville, Utah. "We received newly rebuilt bikes, dolls and dishes, boxing gloves, Chinese checkers and—best of all—a boxer mix puppy that we named Mugs. (I'm on the far right in the bottom right photo.) It was an unforgettable Christmas!"

Unwrap more memories of special teddy bears, electric trains and other toys on the following pages.

window-shopping
wonderland

By Claudine Willis
Portland, Oregon

The J.C. Penney store window lifted the holiday spirits of my friends and me in the midst of the Great Depression in our hometown of Enterprise, Oregon.

When school let out for Christmas break, we bounded out the schoolhouse door. Normally we would have hurried home to play, but it was Christmastime. So, we went sliding on icy sidewalks to Main Street and J.C. Penney to see the store's toy wonderland, a very special sight.

In the center of the display window was a grand Christmas tree covered with so many ornaments that its branches sagged under their weight. Tinfoil icicles tugged the tip of every branch, and strands of beads wove willy-nilly among pretty red-enameled cardinals and frosted bluebirds.

Among other ornaments were miniature horns that really tooted, jingling silver bells and pink pinecones that looked as if they had been dipped in sugar. From the leaning angel on top to the gaudy gold tinsel below, that tree was something to behold!

Beneath the tree, on a bed of white cotton batting, sat myriad toys. It was as if the toy section of the J.C. Penney catalog came to life right before our wondering eyes.

The other girls and I loved looking at the dolls. Their imitation leather shoes tied with satin ribbons peeked out from underneath petticoats trimmed in dainty lace. Of course, each doll had beautiful, curly hair tucked under a ruffled bonnet and the rosiest of cheeks.

Cardboard dollhouses with miniature furniture and china tea sets stood among board games and stacks of storybooks.

The boys loved admiring the flashy red

fire engines, tricycles, wagons and the electric trains complete with station houses and tunnels. There were toy soldiers, Indian drums, cowboy outfits and shootin' guns.

And at the far back of the display was the icing on the cake. There, sleek, varnished sleds stood high on gleaming steel runners. I could just imagine flying down a hill on one of those sleds with the snow whipping at my face.

As the cold settled in around us, we made our way inside the store. We gazed up and down the tall and long shelves of toys until our necks ached.

The Penney's clerks were a lot more patient at Christmastime, and they allowed us to hang around as long as we behaved ourselves. One in particular, Cheryl, looked like a movie star in her marcelled hair, silk blouse and sparkly

Beneath the tree, on a bed of white cotton batting, sat myriad toys. It was as if the toy section of the J.C. Penney catalog came to life right before our wondering eyes.

jewelry. Sometimes she caught us staring at her and would wink and smile back at us.

We always wanted to thank Mr. Penney for his breathtaking window display, but we didn't know where he lived. I asked Mama once, and she said, "Oh, Chicago or New York City or someplace like that." I always wondered why Mr. Penney lived so far away when his store was right here.

Back in those difficult Depression days, most of us kids didn't receive many Christmas gifts, but as Mama said, "Children who get too much don't appreciate anything."

I sure appreciated Mr. Penney's window display. Maybe I couldn't have all the toys in his store, but he gave me something else. He gave me dreams.

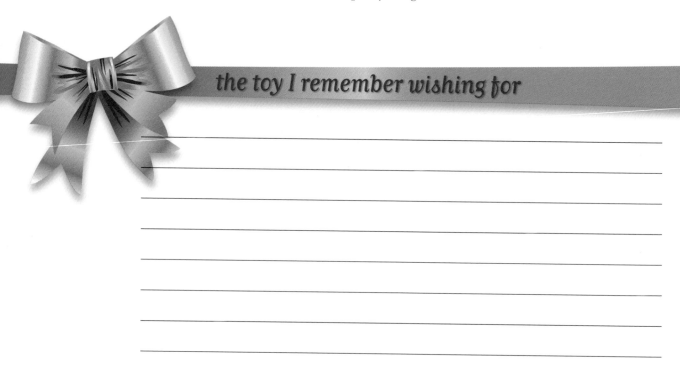

the toy I remember wishing for

_____

_____

_____

_____

_____

_____

_____

"O-OH-H DAD! ...It's a SCHWINN!"

The famous SCHWINN PHANTOM—glistening with more beauty, studded with special features—the finest bicycle in America today!

SCHWINN EXCLUSIVE QUALITY FEATURES
FOR EXTRA VALUE . . . EXTRA PLEASURE

✓ EXCLUSIVE SCHWINN "LOOK"—Smartly designed, richly finished, Schwinn Bicycles are outstanding for beauty. Each evidences Schwinn's long experience.

✓ EXCLUSIVE ELECTRO-FORGED FRAME—Schwinn's own process makes it one continuous steel structure . . . safest, most durable bicycle frame ever built.

✓ EXCLUSIVE "DUR-A-ROL" BEARINGS—Roll easier, last longer. They make possible the effortless pedaling for which Schwinn Bicycles are famous.

✓ EXCLUSIVE TUBULAR RIMS—Special Schwinn construction. Lighter, yet 5-times more rigid than ordinary rims. Built to withstand abuse!

✓ EXCLUSIVE FRONT HUB—Schwinn-made for longer life and easier rolling. Bearings triple-heat-treated for extra-durability.

America's Favorite Bicycles 9 to 1!

This Christmas, Schwinn Bicycles are more than ever the favorite with boys and girls . . . preferred 9 to 1 over any other bike

Your youngster's joy is bound to be greater when the bike you give is a Schwinn . . . because Schwinn is the bike every child wants. Handsome Schwinn Bicycles, with their beautiful colors and many special features so loved by children, are the *preferred* make by far.

The Schwinn name means *quality*—for into these bicycles go the finest materials and the skill of the Schwinn family's 70 years of continuous experience. Schwinn Bicycles are built for extra-safety, built to *last* . . . and backed by a written guarantee that's *honored to the letter!*

You'll find one of the 12,000 Schwinn Authorized Dealers near you. Have him show you today why a Schwinn Bicycle gives more dollar-for-dollar value. Schwinns come in every price class—delivered *ready to ride*. For the best Christmas your youngster ever had—*give a Schwinn!*

IN EVERY PRICE RANGE THERE'S A SCHWINN...THE GUARANTEED BIKE!

ARNOLD, SCHWINN & CO., CHICAGO, ILL.

circa 1951

A Time for Toys

boys and their toys

From trains to trusty steeds, the toys that topped the wish lists of little boys everywhere promised countless hours of action-packed adventure. Hi-Ho, Silver…bells!

▲ Farmer Mike
My son Mike loved his farm toys. In the Christmas of 1958, I bought him a toy tractor just his size. The stick horse leaning against the black-and-white television was one of many. Mike wore out so many stick horses that I started making them out of plastic heads and broomsticks.

— *Lucille Duh, Piscataway, New Jersey*

▲ Sky's the limit
Our sons Tom and Joe were in awe of this Tinker Toy tower that they built with their dad, Joe, during the Christmas season in 1959. It was even taller than the Christmas tree!

— *Joyce Kleefisch*
Sheboygan, Wisconsin

▶ Start your engines
Our son, Joe, 4, was thrilled with his new remote race car set, as you can see by his grin on Christmas morning in 1965. The track even had a double loop!

— *Dolores Kastello*
Waukesha, Wisconsin

▲ **It's a dandy Doody doll**
Here's me with my cat, Bootsie, in front
of my Christmas tree in 1955. I'm holding
my brand-new Howdy Doody doll.

— *Paul Chroniak*
Allenstown, New Hampshire

▼ **What to play with next?**
Our oldest son, Mark, was just over a year old when
this picture was taken on Christmas in 1962. It was
the first Christmas he could really appreciate the
decorated tree and the excitement of opening presents.
Among the toys he received were plastic ABC blocks,
a doll with a baby bottle, an activity center, a small
workbench with hammer and Kittie in the Kegs—seven
colorful nesting barrels with the smallest containing
a cute plastic kitten. My husband, Wayne, and I had
three more boys, so those toys definitely got a workout.
— *Arleen Osvatic, Waukesha, Wisconsin*

Red Ryder hit the mark

In the beloved holiday movie *A Christmas Story*, a tongue-tied
Ralphie Parker finally blurts out to a department store Santa
what he really desires for Christmas: An official Red Ryder,
carbine-action, 200-shot range model air rifle.

Ralphie wasn't alone. During the Daisy Red Ryder's heyday
in the 1930s and '40s, what red-blooded American boy didn't
long to peer down the BB gun's smooth, bore-steel barrel,
and feel that solid wood stock nestled against his shoulder?

Introduced in 1939 and named after a then-popular comic
strip cowboy hero, the Red Ryder model resembled the famed
Winchester repeating rifle—the gun that won the West. Since
then, sales have topped 9 million, despite that near-universal
concern of anguished mothers: "You'll shoot your eye out!"

Clarence Hamilton, a Plymouth Windmill Company
employee, invented the BB gun in 1886. After company
president Lewis Cass Hough took his first shot, he enthused,
"Boy, that's a daisy!" The company soon began making BB guns and toy guns full time and
in 1895 became the Daisy Manufacturing Company Inc.

As for the Red Ryder air gun, it's still sold today—safety glasses not included.

playthings

For children too young to appreciate the holiday season's more meaningful joys, Christmas is all about one thing and one thing only: toys!

While many toys end up as rummage-sale fodder, some remain enduring childhood favorites decades after their introduction. Here's a look at 20 iconic toys introduced over four decades. They are toys that, even today, exhibit extraordinary staying power—and still create especially memorable Christmas mornings.

1930s

Sorry!
Parker Brothers introduced this board game of strategy, luck and good manners in 1934. Since then, generations of families have enjoyed gleefully bumping each other's colored game pieces back to "start"—with sincere apologies, of course.

Monopoly
Who knew real-estate domination, not to mention the thrill of passing Go and collecting $200, could be so much fun? Total sales of this granddaddy of board games have surpassed 250 million sets since Parker Brothers first marketed it in 1935.

View-Master 3-D Viewer
Before global travel became common, millions of

people saw the world through a View-Master 3-D viewer and its reels— circular cardboard discs that hold postcard-like images. Introduced at the New York World's Fair in 1939, the toy has generated sales of more than 1 billion units.

1940s

Slinky
With more than 300 million sold, Slinkys are an American toy institution. Naval mechanical engineer Richard James accidentally invented the toy during World War II while trying to create springs that would keep sensitive instruments stable in rough seas. Richard's wife, Betty, came up with the name, and the couple sold the first Slinkys at Gimbels Department Store in 1945.

Tonka Toys
These virtually indestructible, bright-yellow replicas of construction equipment remain a sandbox staple in backyards everywhere. More than 250 million Tonka Toys (the name means "great" in Dakota-Sioux) have been sold since they debuted in 1947.

Borders: iStockphoto.com/chuwy; View-Master courtesy of Fisher-Price; Mr Potato Head: Spencer Platt/Getty Images

Scrabble

Words can't describe the popularity of this classic game of wordplay, created by unemployed architect Alfred Mosher Butts and trademarked in 1948. More than 100 million sets have sold worldwide. North American consumers alone still buy 1 million to 2 million sets annually.

Candy Land

Americans have been sweet on this game ever since Milton Bradley introduced it in 1949, after recovering polio patient Eleanor Abbot created it for children with the disease. Since then, more than 40 million people have enjoyed trips past the Gumdrop Mountain and through the Peppermint Stick Forest.

1950s

Silly Putty

When General Electric researcher James Wright inadvertently developed a bouncy, pliable substance—made essentially of boric acid and silicone oil—he nicknamed it nutty putty. Consumers went nutty over the novelty item in 1950, when it debuted as Silly Putty, sold in plastic, egg-shape containers.

Mr. Potato Head

The first toy advertised on TV, Mr. Potato Head was the brainchild of inventor George Lerner, who initially sold the concept as a cereal box prize. When introduced by Hasbro in 1952, there was no potato—kids had to use a real spud. A Mrs. Potato Head toy followed in 1953.

Matchbox Cars

In 1953, when Jack Odell learned that his daughter couldn't bring toys to school unless they were small enough to fit inside a matchbox, he made her a tiny brass road roller. Odell's employer, England-based Lesney Products, went on to sell millions of the die-cast metal Matchbox vehicles.

Play-Doh

Moms hate the mess, but kids still can't get enough of Play-Doh, originally invented as a wallpaper remover. Since the pliable, putty-like substance was first marketed as a modeling clay by Noah and Joseph McVicker in 1956, Play-Doh's sales have topped more than 2 billion cans.

Frisbee

California carpenter Walter Frederick Morrison transformed summer picnics and backyard barbecues forever when he invented the Frisbee (which he called the Pluto Platter), introduced by the Wham-O toy company in 1957. The name Frisbee can be traced to the Frisbie Baking Company, which made pies that were sold to many New England colleges. College students enjoyed playing catch with the empty pie plates, which were stamped "Frisbie."

Hula Hoop

The Wham-O toy company prompted a whole lot of hip-shakin' when it introduced the brightly colored plastic hula hoop in 1958. In the first year alone, consumers snapped up more than 100 million at $1.98 apiece.

1960s

Etch a Sketch

This timeless toy is one of the few blockbusters of its era that hasn't changed much since it debuted in 1960. Sporting its distinctive red frame, the mesmerizing Etch a Sketch still relies on two knobs

that, when twisted, move a stylus mounted on a pair of rails. The stylus etches black lines in a fine aluminum powder that sticks to the toy's glass screen.

LEGO® Bricks

Created by Danish carpenter-turned-toymaker Ole Kirk Christiansen, plastic LEGO building blocks have kindled children's imaginations since they hit toy stores in the United States in 1961. The LEGO Company (the name derives from the first two letters of the Danish words *leg godt*, which means "play well") has produced more than 400 billion LEGO blocks—and counting.

Easy-Bake Oven

Pretend play for aspiring young cooks quickly became blasé in 1963, when Kenner Products introduced the Easy-Bake Oven, a working oven powered by a lightbulb.

G.I. Joe

Introduced by Hasbro in 1964, G.I. Joe made dolls—and their accessories—cool for young boys. Conceived by toy creator Stan Weston as a Barbie for boys, G.I. Joe (the name comes from a World War II slang term for soldiers; the G.I. stands for "government issue") continues to evolve even today.

Twister

Milton Bradley first sold this classic party game—which uses humans as game pieces—in 1966. The company sold more than 3 million games in the first year alone, boosted by *Tonight Show* host Johnny Carson, who played the game on television with guest Eva Gabor.

Battleship

"You sunk my battleship!" is still a familiar refrain in family rooms nationwide, just as it was in 1967 when Milton Bradley introduced this iconic board game of strategic, hit-or-miss guesswork.

Hot Wheels

Few things made young boys' hearts beat faster than Hot Wheels die-cast metal race cars, which Mattel debuted in 1968. Designed to compete with Matchbox cars, Hot Wheels upped the ante with low-frictions wheels that allowed the cars to travel 200 miles per hour—in 1:64 scale, of course. Hot Wheels' sales surpassed 2 billion units in 1998.

circa 1958

girls & dolls

From their Dy-Dee dolls to their tiny tea sets, little girls are sweet reminders of the season's softer side. And these reader stories are proof that Christmas fairy tales do come true!

▶ Cowgirl power

My cousin Rose Mary King and I received cowgirl outfits for Christmas in 1958. We dressed up and posed with our dolls (hers in blue, mine in pink), which we also got for Christmas, at my dad's grocery store, King's Super Market, in Pikeville, Kentucky.

— *Lynden King Spears*
Pikeville, Kentucky

◀ Industrious little lady

My daughter Michele always wanted to iron when I did. So for Christmas of 1969, when she was 3, Santa brought Michele her very own ironing board and iron. Of course, she immediately snatched up a shirt so she could start putting her gift to good use.

— *Louise LaMarca-Gay*
Rochester, New Hampshire

▶ Best present ever

Some kids really did get a pony for Christmas, as Julie Hoffman Johnson discovered in 1946. The present was from her grandpa when they lived in Michigan, says Julie, who now resides in Evansville, Indiana.

▼ Early delivery

My family always went to church on Christmas Eve. In 1950, when we returned from church that year, the tree was ablaze with twinkling Christmas lights. My brother, who was supposedly at work, had been busy while we were gone. In the middle of the pile of gifts was "Sweetie Pie," a doll with curly red hair and blue eyes, dressed in a silky pink dress and bonnet. Sweetie Pie nestled in bed with me that very night. She became my best friend and forever my favorite doll.

— *Ellen G. King*
Hilliards, Pennsylvania

▲ A busy elf

My daddy always loved creating masterpieces in his basement workshop. Because he didn't have any loud power tools in the 1930s, my sister, Evelyn, and I never knew when he was working. Each year, after church, we could expect gifts under the Christmas tree. Daddy always had something new for us girls that he had crafted in his shop. One year, my family and I were walking to Christmas Mass when Dad turned back to see if he had "left a light on." We came home to find a beautiful hand-crafted table and set of chairs, complete with a china tea set. We immediately invited our dolls over for a Christmas tea party.

— *Dolores Crilly, Fort Wayne, Indiana*

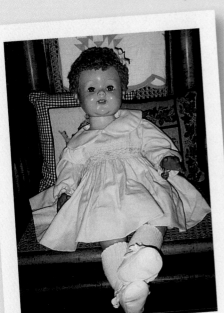

Hey, doll face!

From Shirley Temple to Barbie,
dolls remain a girl's best friend.

Just as surely as Santa wears red, dolls stand atop many a little girl's Christmas wish list. But the kinds of dolls they've desired over the decades have been as varied as Barbie's wardrobe.

One constant from the 1920s to the present is the **Madame Alexander doll**, created by Beatrice Alexander Behrman, who founded the Alexander Doll Co. in 1923. Madame Alexander dolls were industry pioneers; a list of firsts includes dolls based on licensed cinema and literary figures; dolls with eyes that open and close; and the first "full-figured fashion" doll, aka Cissy (circa 1955).

In the 1930s, **Shirley Temple dolls**—one of the first celebrity dolls—set girls' hearts aflutter, as did Nancy Ann dolls, created by Nancy Ann Abbott in 1936.

The Vogue Doll Company's **Ginny dolls**, named after creator Jennie Grave's daughter, Virginia, took girldom by storm during the 1950s, as did **Sweet Sue dolls**, which were made by the American Character Doll Co.

But the 1959 launch of shapely, perky **Barbie** set the benchmark for all dolls irretrievably high. Mattel Inc. co-founder Ruth Handler created the 11½-inch-tall plastic fashion plate, named after her daughter, and the doll world has never been the same. With more than 1 billion sold and annual sales that often exceed $1 billion, Barbie is bound to be a fixture on Christmas wish lists for years to come.

paging through memories

Do these toys from the 1941 Montgomery Ward Christmas Book ring merry memory bells for you? Thanks to Clayton Smith of Norfolk, Virginia, for sharing the pages!

a memory for the long haul

By Larry Fast, Salem, Oregon

I was 5½ years old in the fall of 1952. My grand desire for Christmas that year was a toy log truck—no doubt inspired by the heavy logging industry in northwest Oregon, where I lived.

At our home, presents were wrapped and placed under the tree long before Christmas day. A certain large box wrapped in red-and-white-striped paper garnered my attention early. Almost every night I would lie down beside it, the twinkling Christmas lights above me, and dream and scheme about my ultimate toy.

Sure enough, Christmas morning yielded a beautiful yellow and green Timber Toter log truck made by the All American Toy Co. of Salem, Oregon, established in 1947. It was a quality-made truck with an aluminum cab; solid, soft rubber tires on pivotal axles; and a hood-mounted air horn that steered the truck. It drove forward, backward and around corners, just like a real truck. I spent many pleasure-filled hours playing with that very special toy.

The log-hauling bed eventually evolved into other uses. My dad fashioned some light plywood to make it a long flatbed hauler for my other equipment and goods. That log truck kept me well entertained until about the age of 12. And while I eventually moved on to other interests, I thank my dad for a most wonderful "dream-come-true" Christmas.

WISH COME TRUE Larry Fast proudly shows off his new log truck at Christmastime of 1952. Next to him is his sister, Lynette, with her new doll.

the toy I wish I still had

all I want for Christmas

Two readers share their heartwarming—and humorous—letters to Santa.

▶ I was 6 or 7 when I entered a contest the weekly newspaper of our little Iowa town had for writing the best letter to Santa. I won the contest. The prize? A sled!

— *Joyce Appleton Jackson*
Sarasota, Florida

▼ I found this handwritten note among my mother's things. It was in her handwriting and was, obviously, dictated to her by my brother Andy. Reading it brings back memories of the magic we felt as children in the '50s. Anything was possible—if you asked Santa!

— *Kay Elmore*
Millington, Illinois

Dear Santa,
I am just asking for a few things because I don't want to be selfish. Will you please bring me a sled, stockings and a pair of shoes? When you come to my house and look under the Christmas tree, you'll find candy and nuts. Help yourself. Come early, before my Daddy eats it all.
Your little friend,
Joyce Appleton

Dear Santa,
Please bring me "Trigger" or another wild horse to tame. I am four years old. My sister, Kay, is three and wants a doll. My brother, Bill, can't think of anything he needs. I am good... sometimes.

Andy, 1950

IN THE SPIRIT Kay Nord Elmore and brothers Andy Nord (center) and Bill Hollaway in '54.

doggone good
Christmas

It was the Christmas of 1956 when my brother, Jimmy, and I got our mechanical dogs. They were battery-operated and ran across the floor, stopping every so often to sit up on their haunches and bark. Here we are with our mother, Martina. I'm holding one of the dogs, and Jimmy (notice the coon-skin cap) is posing with his new cash register—you won't find that on many wish lists today!

— *Joan Meyer, Grand Rapids, Michigan*

CHAPTER ELEVEN

Stocking Stuffers

Ah, what's more exciting than the first peek into a Christmas stocking to glimpse the treasures inside? "My stocking was the very best part of Christmas," recalls Nanette Wells of Sheffield, Massachusetts. "In the late 1940s through early '50s, it awaited me each Christmas morning brimful. I always found an orange in the toe, miniature Hershey bars, Christmas hard candy, mixed nuts in the shell and a candy cane or two. Often there was a jar of sweet pickles—one of my favorites, but not a family one.

"There was usually a small toy or two, and then a book of paper dolls or a coloring book with a box of crayons or colored pencils. Sometimes one of the treasures was a historical book of buildings and people to cut out and assemble. Also nestled inside I might find other surprises, like a small flashlight, a box of Cracker Jack, a kaleidoscope, a magic trick, or a tube of gunk with a small straw for blowing little plastic balloons. But no single item within matched all the special magic that always reached out from the top of that wonderfully stuffed stocking."

Turn the page to see what surprises you'll find in this chapter—stories that are sweet, delightful or touched with the unexpected.

bring on the balloons

By Joe Kleefisch
Sheboygan, Wisconsin

There was a chill in the air that Saturday after Thanksgiving in 1952, so my wife and I bundled up our daughter before we took her outside. It was the day of the Christmas parade in downtown Sheboygan, and Mary, 1½, would be seeing it for the first time.

Joyce, Mary and I found a spot along the 1½-mile parade route on the corner of Ninth and Michigan, then watched and clapped as local bands and marching units passed by. But nothing captured our attention as much as the big balloon floats that slowly made their way toward us.

Big, colorful balloons were towed by cars or pulled along the street by local boys dressed as clowns.

We watched in amazement as a 75-foot-long float of Santa in his sleigh—pulled by nine life-size reindeer—flew by us. We'd never seen anything like it. Next came a tall Christmas tree with lights, a grinning snowman, an immense candy cane, an elephant, a sea serpent, an ice cream cone and a Humpty Dumpty—each more surprising than the last.

The parade lasted more than an hour. And when it was over, we walked to the H.C. Prange's on North Eighth Street to join other spectators in front of the store's beautiful window displays. Like the other children gathered there, Mary was entranced by the animated figures. With the fanciful parade balloons looming large in our minds, it was a memorable way to start the holiday season that year.

GROS' AIRY ART FORMS APPEARED ACROSS THE COUNTRY

Christmas parades showcasing the amazing balloon confections of Pittsburgh's Jean Gros were seen by millions in the late 1940s and into the '50s. Hundreds of towns of all sizes staged parades featuring the colorfully painted balloons each year during the six-week parade season, Nov. 1 to Dec. 15.

Inspired by the giant balloons at Macy's parade in New York City, Gros wanted to fashion smaller versions for parades in small towns everywhere. To do that, he needed to make the balloons less than 15 feet tall, so they could move beneath overhead wires. Because helium was expensive, the balloons had to be inflated with air. They also had to be easy to deflate, pack and transport.

Gros managed to accomplish all that while designing a host of unusual characters made of rubberized fabric—from pigs, horses and kangaroos to prehistoric creatures, dragons and monsters. His fanciful forms played a big part in the holiday celebrations of millions of people.

FESTIVE FLOATS Like parades across the country, the Christmas parade in Sheboygan, Wisconsin, in November 1952 starred the colorful balloon creations of Jean Gros. The parade featured more than 40 large balloons, including a float of Santa and his sleigh—valued at $10,000 at the time—followed by a 14-foot Christmas tree (top), a smiling snowman (middle) and a two-headed creature (bottom).

better than any toy

By Arlene Lewis, Warren, Ohio

I was 4 years old on that snowy Christmas Eve in 1929. All the kids were sent off to bed early in our big old house with no electricity and no central heat. I scrunched under the covers on my little cot at the far side of the living room and was soon fast asleep. But only a bit later I felt someone shaking me awake. It was my big brother, Charles, telling me to go upstairs for the rest of the night.

Only half-awake, I trudged up the stairs and crawled into the big bed with sisters Norma and Dorothy. I pulled the mound of blankets up over my head, leaving a small opening for my nose to poke out and breathe in the frosty air. I was sound asleep when, again, someone shook me to wake up. It was morning, and there was Charles, telling me to go downstairs. I inched one bare foot and then the other out onto the icy floor and scrambled down the stairs, my two sisters in hot pursuit.

The first thing I saw as I reached the bottom of the stairs was a strange little creation sitting on the big round dining room table. About 18 inches high, it had eight skinny wire branches covered in green fuzz stretching out in every direction. I knew it was a Christmas tree because it had eight skinny strands of tinfoil draped over the top. I didn't know where it came from, but I thought, *Wow, we never had such a Christmas tree like that before!*

Then I noticed Dad standing at the kitchen stove and stirring something in a huge pot. He was cooking our breakfast of lumpy oatmeal. He turned, and with a happy smile and a twinkle in his eye, instructed us all to go into the bedroom, where Mom had a surprise for us. Full of curiosity, we edged our way into the room, and there was Mom, still in bed. Cradled in her arms was the most beautiful baby in the whole wide world. We stared in awe as she announced, "This is your new baby brother. His name is Richard."

I didn't know where he came from or how he got there—in those days small children did not know when their mother was expecting a baby—but I thought, *Wow, we never had a Christmas present like this before!*

This was better than all the toys in Woolworth's. You got tired of playing with the same old toys and just stuck them under the bed. I would never get tired of playing with my new little brother, and I would certainly never just stick him under the bed!

As we grew older, Richard and I became buddies, sharing adventures and spending many long, hot summer days together. Years later, I can say I was right that Christmas morning long ago. My brother Richard has proved to be better than any Christmas toy, for he's a very special person in my life 365 days a year.

troublesome trade

My mother, Eileen Bell King, was 2½ years old and living in Berwyn, Illinois, when this picture was taken in 1925. She got this beautiful Cadillac pedal car for Christmas but apparently wasn't impressed, because she traded it for a ride on another child's tricycle. The Caddy was never found, and she got into big trouble!

— *Jackie Gruesbeck, Perry, Michigan*

literary surprise

I was 16 at Christmastime 1940 and had asked my parents for the book *Parnassus on Wheels* by Christopher Morley. On Christmas morning, instead of my usual pile of gifts under the tree, I found one small present. That led to a treasure hunt all over the house and, finally, to the garage. There I found my book—on the red leather seat of a beautiful powder-blue 1941 Oldsmobile convertible. Set into both sides of the hood were my initials in chrome. One button raised and lowered the top and another set off a horn that played *In My Merry Oldsmobile*. I named the car "Parnassus on Wheels," Nassy for short. I no longer have the car, but I do have the book.

— *Margaret Davis, Alamosa, Colorado*

merry mishap

Santa's sense of humor

My favorite Christmas memory is from the early 1930s in Greenfield, Massachusetts. Santa gave us unusually large gifts that didn't fit in our stockings. A long ribbon led from my stocking to a BB gun, and another went from my brother's stocking to a wicker doll carriage. We spent hours conjecturing whether Santa was in such a hurry that he made a mistake or whether he had a sense of humor.

—*Shirley Corse, Scarsborough, Maine*

golden discovery

In the 1950s, when I was in third grade, I chose a Christmas tree tall enough to reach the ceiling in our living room in Sawyer, Oklahoma. My dad thought it was too big, but I begged him to cut it down. Unfortunately, we had so few ornaments that the tree was mostly bare, and I knew there was no money to buy more.

When I went into the kitchen to ask my mother if she would pop some corn to string, I saw something that took my breath away. Sitting on the kitchen table were the most gorgeous, shiny Christmas decorations I had ever seen. They were big, and they were golden! I gathered up my new decorations by the armload and started decorating the tree.

I was so proud of that tree, and every day I would move some of my lovely gold decorations to different places on the tree. I even added a few from my grandmother's house. Wherever I went, I would invite everyone to come and see my tree.

Later, I learned those beautiful golden decorations were jar rings and lids that my mother used for canning fruits and vegetables. And if you come to my house this year, you will find a gold jar ring and jar lid on it.

— *Judie Garner Brunson, Wichita Falls, Texas*

building a rapport with Santa

My grandpap, Joseph Ranker, worked as a carpenter for Kaufmann's Department Store in downtown Pittsburgh for more than 30 years. He was sent to repair something in Santaland one day and started clowning around with Santa Claus. Both were in a good mood, since the holidays were close at hand and Kaufmann's was a great place to work. This picture *(right)*, taken in the 1950s, is the result.

In those days, carpenters and tradesmen had a strict dress code: white overalls, blue or white oxford shirt, a tie and cap. Kaufmann's had 11 floors, and carpenters were constantly building and tearing down displays. You can see the hammer in my grandpap's hand.

My grandpap had the distinction of working on Frank Lloyd Wright's historic Fallingwater, built as a home for Edgar Kaufmann, the owner of Kaufmann's. As a cost-cutting move, Mr. Kaufmann used his own store carpenters rather than contractors to complete the inside finish work.

Now for a coincidence: Not only have I worked as a carpenter in that very same store, but some 50 years later, I am now the Santa Claus for the store, which is now Macy's.

— *John Suhr, Pittsburgh, Pennsylvania*

beehives & biscuits

Every time I see this photo of my mother and her two sisters, it makes me laugh. It was taken on Christmas Eve 1970 and shows (from left) my aunt Connie Senter Rains; my mom, Patricia Ann Senter Faircloth; and my aunt Virgia Senter Avery with their magnificent beehive hairdos. They're each holding a bag of Snow Flake flour, a gift from their father. Most "Southern ladies" know how to make biscuits, but evidently my mother and aunts didn't practice that skill very often. So my grandfather decided to give them a little push, buying them each a biscuit tray and a small bag of flour! From their expressions, they seem less than thrilled with their gifts.

— *Angie Norris*
Fuquay-Varina, North Carolina

ring a bell?

Do you remember the Norelco TV commercials with Santa riding the floating heads of an electric shaver over the hills of snow? The ad campaign, which started in the 1960s, used stop-action animation and was so popular that it continued for decades.

nutty way to learn the truth

A few days before Christmas 1962, I went grocery shopping with my father. We were choosing candy and nuts when I asked him why we needed these supplies. As I studied an oddly shaped peanut that I tossed into the bag, Dad gave me a noncommittal answer.

When Christmas Day arrived, I found that unusually shaped peanut in my stocking! At 8, I was old enough to put two and two together. I finished opening my presents, a little startled, but still happy for my goodies. Later, as my mother prepared the Christmas meal, I asked for confirmation of my revelation. She gave me a straightforward answer, which I appreciated.

Though believing in Santa was wonderful, I remember feeling grown up and quite wise when I realized the truth. And now I look back on my enlightenment with a smile.

— *Leslie Chilton, Tempe, Arizona*

how I learned the truth about Santa

a classic Christmas rediscovered

I recently found this 8x10 photo that was made of me on Christmas 1925 in Nashville, Tennessee. I was 1½ at the time, so I don't remember any of the gifts that year. But from the look of things, there were quite a few toys, and I'm sure I enjoyed them! My father became a photographer during World War I. When he returned, he taught his youngest brother how to make and develop photographs, so either of them could have taken this picture. In any case, it was hand-tinted and has kept well these many years.

— *Stanley Hime, Brentwood, Tennessee*